"In recent years, new terms have entered the vocabulary of both the Southern Baptist Convention and the evangelical world. These include words like critical race theory, intersectionality, social justice, and woke. Often people discuss and argue over these terms without truly understanding either their denotations or connotations. Others clearly know the meaning of the terms and reject being labeled by them altogether. Still, others know exactly what they mean and embrace them. Since the tragic death of George Floyd, these discussions have increased exponentially. With the ubiquitous discussions, confusion has also increased. If we are to move forward, we must have a clear word on the issues at hand. That is exactly what Ronnie Rogers has provided for us in *A Corruption of Consequence: Adding Social Justice to the Gospel*. Ronnie addresses the issues at hand in a straightforward, benevolent, and respectful tone. Whether you are simply wondering what the fuss is all about, or if you are engaged in the discussion on one side or the other, this volume is a must-read. Thank you, Ronnie Rogers, for a clear word on these issues that threaten to divide us!"

—**MARK H. BALLARD**
President/Founder, Northeastern Baptist College

"The adoption of Resolution 9 at the 2019 annual meeting of the Southern Baptist Convention took place in a mostly empty convention center as the meeting concluded. Few Southern Baptists were present, and even fewer understood what was being proposed. Although that event proved to be one of the most controversial of the decade, still, few evangelicals understand what is behind critical race theory, social justice, and intersectionality. I rejoiced when *A Corruption of Consequence* by Ronnie Rogers came across my desk. He adeptly explains these terms and why they should concern Christians—making his case entirely from the sufficiency of Scripture. Rogers has led his congregation through understanding the matters he presents in this work, and now his careful study and biblical critique are available for all. If I were to read only one book this year, this would, without a doubt, be the one. Christians desiring to understand the truth about the challenges facing our nation and evangelicalism cannot afford to miss *A Corruption of Consequence*."

—**Z. SCOTT COLTER**
Executive Director, Sandy Creek Foundation,
and Co-founder, Conservative Baptist Network

"*A Corruption of Consequence* is a must-read for anyone who wants to understand the causes of our national confusion. Ronnie Rogers is a pastoral scholar who wields the truth of a biblical worldview as a spiritual hammer with which he shatters the lie that a Christian can embrace 'social justice' and critical race theory without destroying the basic teachings of Christ. For Southern Baptists, this is a wonderful clarification. Settling this issue will allow Southern Baptists to reclaim their Convention and again become an effective witness to the world."

—TOM HATLEY
Pastor, IBC Global Outreach Center

"The social justice agenda is both seductive and deceptive: seductive because all people of good will—especially Christians—long for justice and reconciliation for all—yet deceptive because social justice (as opposed to actual justice) offers the very opposite of both. It defines one group as incapable of redemption, even for acts it never committed, and another as incapable of needing it. It is the antithesis of the gospel, which recognizes all as sinners, and redemption as available to all on equal terms beneath the cross. Ronnie Rogers is one of the Southern Baptists' greatest leaders and pastors. His highly accessible primer on this otherwise complex topic is a vital tool for a church increasingly awash in the philosophies of this world and bereft of the simple gospel. It is not just a must-read, but an urgent one."

—ROD D. MARTIN
Founder and CEO, The Martin Organization, Inc.,
and SBC Executive Committee member

A Corruption of Consequence

A Corruption of Consequence

Adding Social Justice to the Gospel

Ronnie W. Rogers

Foreword by Paige Patterson

RESOURCE *Publications* · Eugene, Oregon

A CORRUPTION OF CONSEQUENCE
Adding Social Justice to the Gospel

Resource Publications
An Imprint of Wipf and Stock Publishers
199 W. 8th Ave., Suite 3
Eugene, OR 97401

www.wipfandstock.com

PAPERBACK ISBN: 978-1-7252-9538-4
HARDCOVER ISBN: 978-1-7252-9537-7
EBOOK ISBN: 978-1-7252-9539-1

02/19/21

Scripture quotations taken from the NEW American Standard Bible (NASB)

I lovingly dedicate this book to my sixth grandson, Leo Rockwell Heinrich, and my first granddaughter, Louisa DuBois Heinrich. Leo, I have been waiting for you, and I am proud that you bear your great grandfather's name; he would be proud as well. Louisa, you are the granddaughter for whom I have been waiting a long time; that you bear the name, DuBois, from your Aunt Nancy, is supra special. I pray this book will, one day, help you both to learn and understand Scripture so you can follow Christ and speak his truth to the world. For that is where you will experience life at its fullest. You are immeasurably special to me, and I love you, Leo Rockwell and Louisa DuBois.

Contents

Foreword

IF MY WIFE DOROTHY had been a sailor, she would not have been charmed by the siren songs that wrecked mythical ships falling prey to Scylla or Charybdis in the Strait of Messina. Her immunity to such wind chimes, however, is not extended to sermons. A preacher who delivers a thoughtful, theologically accurate, impassioned message never fails to gain her attention and approval. Fortunately for me, a message will leap to my phone stating something to the effect of, "listen to this sermon if you want to be both enlightened and spiritually sustained!" Recently, she transmitted to me an entire sermon series preached by Pastor Ronnie Rogers of Trinity Baptist Church in Norman, Oklahoma. Contemporary cultural Marxism was the theme of the series, a topic that previously had the effect of curing any insomnia I ever experienced. I knew Ronnie Rogers to be an outstanding, consistent expositor of God's word, and I could scarcely imagine him as an "eristic preacher" taking on the demons of any era. But knowing that we would certainly dine the next morning on eggs, coffee, and Rogers' messages, I decided the best course of action was immediately to listen to these sermons.

That decision was one of the best of my life. I later wrote to Pastor Rogers, insisting that in addition to internet access, the churches and the people of God needed to see these messages in print. Consequently, I am delighted to hold in my hand *A Corruption of Consequence: Adding Social Justice to the Gospel* From the beginning of Rogers' ministry at Trinity Baptist Church, located near the University of Oklahoma, he has exhibited the research of a true scholar. This monograph is no exception. Evangelicals have recently been confronted with critical race theory and intersectionality. Other forms of cultural Marxism have lifted their heads. Southern Baptists were asked to endorse Resolution Nine at the 2019 annual meeting of the Southern Baptist Convention even though the terms and ideologies espoused in the resolution were foreign to the average Baptist. What exactly is "cultural Marxism"? Is it dangerous to our churches, and does it represent a departure from our confidence in the sufficiency of Scripture as a guide to faith and practice? Ronnie Rogers understands the intricacies of Marxism and its abysmal universal failures. And he grasps the mutations of Marxism championed by so many of the universities of our day. He fathoms the depths of critical race theory and the isolationism of intersectionality. And more importantly, as an accomplished theologian, Pastor Rogers knows why "cultural Marxism" is not congruent in any fashion with the biblical theology of Evangelicals.

One of the most remarkable aspects of this monograph is that even though it bears the marks of the finest scholarship available, the book is nonetheless a garland of literary splendor, written with a determination to address the thoughts and affections of those who have not been blessed with opportunities to gain familiarity with the philosophical world. A congregant in one of our churches who loves Christ, the Bible, and men of every race will be able to comprehend the words of truth that are so resplendent in the pages of this volume.

In *A Corruption of Conscience*, Rogers calls the names of advocates of these novel positions. But he does so in typical "Rogerian" style. Because he has the heart of a loving pastor, even when he disagrees with individuals, he stipulates his position shrouded in love and understanding. Aware of his own inadequacies, Rogers delineates the positions of others with caution and without exaggeration. Then, in keeping with his role as "pastor-prophet," he calls the church to repentance and to return to a stand for truth. "Biblical justice" is preferred above "social justice."

Following thirteen incisive chapters, Rogers provides five critical appendices. The culmination of the book is a superb bibliography consisting of sources illuminating all sides of the issues discussed, once again demonstrating the fairness and objectivity of this pastor's approach. Containing both a subject index and an invaluable scriptural index, this book lends itself not only to general reading but also to the scholarly endeavor.

Respectfully engaging well-known Baptists like Russell Moore, Albert Mohler, Jarvis Williams, Matthew Hall, Curtis Woods, and Danny Akin, Rogers exemplifies how to sustain a debate without forfeiting one's Christianity. If there were ever a day when the church needed a book like this one, it is now. This monograph, penned by a pastor-scholar, is one that every pastor needs to read. And the people of Zion's churches

Foreword

can grasp its message easily. Purchase the book and read its words with a heart seeking preparation to deal with the cultural challenges facing our world today.

Paige Patterson
President, Sandy Creek Foundation
Dallas, Texas

Preface

I BELIEVE THE PRESENT emphasis on social justice and critical race theory, rather than biblical justice, disparages all humans by treating them as something less than they are, which is created in the image of God (Gen 1:26–28). First, this current emphasis is based on a Marxian materialistic view of reality. Second, this perspective categorizes white and black people as oppressors and oppressed based on skin color rather than on their hearts as God judges them (1 Sam 16:7).

Third, social justice degrades black people by contending that their lack of achievement can be blamed on others (social injustice) rather than considering other factors not associated with social injustices. As with a white person, a black person's lack of accomplishment can be the result of such factors as a lack of personal responsibility, poor work ethic, and socially inherited attitudes. It can also be affected by factors beyond their control that are not the product of racism, such as geography, parental dynamic, or familial and cultural value systems. These and many other factors can affect outcomes for both blacks and whites.

While there have been times in which the lack of accomplishment of blacks was due to racial injustice such as with slavery and to a lesser, although significant, degree post-slavery agreements made by whites to keep blacks down and the Jim Crow laws, that is not descriptive of our current society. It has not been true since the gains of the civil rights movement.[1] Blacks and whites are both equally image-bearers of God and can, therefore, choose to act responsibly or irresponsibly with the freedoms they have.[2]

1. This is not a denial of individual prejudice toward others, which can be found in every race. It is, however, as many black conservatives contend, a denial that those prejudices are sufficient to stop a person from being successful in personal development and life.

2. Some of the same problems such as black on black crime and out of wedlock

Further, while the continued presence of areas of racism makes their success more difficult than for others who do not have to contend with that obstacle, that does not mean others do not have significant barriers to overcome. They may even have greater ones or more of them, such as severe physical handicaps, mental deficiencies, worse socially inherited assumptions, inferior geographical locations, or more prohibitive familial experiences. Lastly, in our present era, many blacks advance to either equal or surpass their white counterparts, which evidences that more is at play than just social injustices when a black person fails to progress. That is to say, unequal outcomes do not necessarily evidence the presence of injustices.

On a personal note, I would like to say that my nephew, whom we raised for several years, married a black girl with my blessings, and they have three children; as a result, I am happily the great uncle of a biracial great-niece and two great-nephews. I have performed marital counseling for biracial couples and performed biracial (black and white) weddings. The church where I have pastored for over twenty-two years is composed of ten different races. Our associate pastor adopted four black children, and our worship pastor adopted five black-American, two Haitian, one Hispanic, and two Korean children.

There is no other church on earth that I would rather pastor. Also, I think I am safe to say that no one would desire to be a member of our church if they were an actual racist. And yet, according to critical race theory and Black Lives Matter, all of the white people in our church are racists. This includes our associate pastor and worship leader. The Bible says differently.

Ronnie W. Rogers

---

pregnancy exist in areas governed by black and liberal leaders, city councils, mayors, police chiefs, and governors. Yet, many blacks in these and worse situations choose to act responsibly and excel.

Acknowledgments

MOST OF ALL, I thank Jesus for the work he has done in my life. I thank Gina, my wife, confidante, friend, and co-laborer in life and ministry, who has made the greatest impact upon my life other than Jesus.

I would also like to thank Larry Toothaker and Billy Wolfe for their gracious willingness to proof my manuscript and provide invaluable insights; Anita Charlson for tirelessly and professionally editing this manuscript; J. R. Crosby for the cover design; Trinity's elders for their unwavering support of my commitment to study and their steadfast encouragement for me to equip the saints and write; as well as the fellowship and support of my brothers and sisters in Trinity Baptist Church whom I have been blessed beyond measure to serve for twenty-two years. You have loved me without measure and provided me the greatest opportunity for spiritual growth. My longevity as your pastor is a testimony of your Christ-like gracious and generous forbearing love towards me. No man could deserve such a life of being loved, but none so little as me.

I will live and die indebted to all of you for your love and support.

1

What Does Social Justice and
Critical Race Theory Mean for Me?

YOU MAY BE WONDERING what do things like social justice and critical race theory mean for me? Do they matter to my family, the work of the kingdom, and the gospel? Although you may be unfamiliar with these topics, this book is designed to make these subjects and their importance understandable in light of the Scripture and the gospel. You will see how these issues affect not only your life but your children and their children as well.

I intend to define and explain in an understandable manner how issues such as critical theory,[1] critical race theory,[2] and intersectionality,[3] which are part of what is known as cultural Marxism, do affect us and the

---

1. Both critical race theory and cultural Marxism are a part of critical theory. Critical theory seeks to change society rather than just explain it like other social theories. When someone uses critical theory, they presume there are oppressors and those that are oppressed. James Bohman says, "A theory is critical to the extent that it seeks human "emancipation from slavery," and acts as a "liberating . . . influence" (Horkheimer 1972, 246) . . . such theories aim to explain and transform all the circumstances that enslave human beings." Bohman, "Critical Theory," para. 1.

2. Critical race theory is "the view that race, instead of being biologically grounded and natural, is socially constructed and that race, as a socially constructed concept, functions as a means to maintain the interests of the white population that constructed it." Curry, "Critical Race Theory," para. 1.

3. Intersectionality is defined in the Oxford Dictionary as "The interconnected nature of social categorizations such as race, class, and gender as they apply to a given individual or group, regarded as creating overlapping and interdependent systems of discrimination or disadvantage." See "Intersectionality." Consequently, minorities can suffer from varying degrees of discrimination.

gospel of our Savior.[4] We must work toward understanding these deadly concepts because they have moved from secular academia, our government entities,[5] and the identity politics of Democrats to evangelicalism and the Southern Baptist Convention (SBC).[6]

Since cultural Marxism and social justice have substantial similarities, they can often be used interchangeably.[7] For example, both advocate anarchist tactics, both advocate socialism or communism and are against capitalism, their view of justice conflicts with biblical justice, and they believe in the redistribution of wealth and power by force in order to usher in a socialistic Utopia. Since social justice is the most well-known term, I will use it whenever it is unnecessary to mention cultural Marxism, or there is a need to clarify a particular trait of critical theory, critical race theory, or intersectionality.[8]

Here are a couple of emphases and outcomes of these ideas that will highlight their importance to all of us. Cultural Marxism says the world is made up of oppressors and the oppressed. Critical race theory teaches that all white people are privileged white supremacists and oppressors because they are the majority and white. Black people, being the minority, are oppressed. The whites need to repent of privilege and racism. But they cannot effectively repent and change since they are the majority who created widespread racism, and they will always be white. Blacks do not need to repent because, being a minority, they cannot be racist.[9]

---

4. Cultural Marxism broadly encompasses better-known terms like critical race theory, intersectionality, social justice, and is the fountainhead of identity politics. Cultural Marxism proposes a clash between the oppressed (minorities) and the oppressor (majority). The "majority groups are typically defined as privileged and oppressive, with minority groups accordingly labeled underprivileged and oppressed." Thenewcalvinist, "Stain," 9:36–44.

5. Rufo, "Summary of Critical Race Theory."

6. I will explain these concepts in greater detail in the rest of this book. I will contrast each major component of cultural Marxism with the Scripture.

7. Although they are not synonymous.

8. Some of the questions regarding social justice are what is included in the term, what are its historical and present connections, and how is the term commonly used? Some ideas under the social justice umbrella are not in and of themselves inherently problematic. For example, concepts like equality and the common good are not necessarily problematic. The problem arises when people begin to define these terms and explain how they achieve them. A wide array of social justice proponents promote socialism, if not Marxism, under the banner of social justice. The few who seek to separate social justice from its Marxian nature seek to explain the term more narrowly than can be legitimately done.

9. Some would disagree that minorities cannot be racist, but, generally, that is not the

According to critical theory, this same prescription applies to various sets of social groups where there are majorities and minorities. Heterosexuals, the majority, are the oppressors of homosexuals, the minority and the oppressed. Cisgenders (people who identify with their birth sex) are the majority, and therefore the oppressors of transgender people, the minority.

Intersectionality teaches that a person can experience multilevel discrimination. Consequently, a black woman could experience discrimination on two levels (being a woman and black). Identifying with more minority groups increases discrimination. For example, a black lesbian could experience it on three levels. The more levels of discrimination one experiences, the more authoritative and believable their understanding, claims, and opinions become.

Intersectionality is, by its nature, divisive since it creates multiple identities for people based on their understanding of discrimination against them, minority status, which by their nature, separates people into small groups. Communication between groups is hindered because the level of access to grasping truth is dependent on how many intersecting discriminations the individual believes he has suffered; thus, the basis of identity politics.

In contrast, white people, especially white men, are privileged, and therefore their truth claims have little or no merit or authority. That is to say, truth claims by the oppressors are suspect until proven true. In contrast, the truth claims by the oppressed are reliable until proven wrong, which intersectionality makes almost impossible since only the oppressed can understand the real truth; the majority who are the oppressors cannot.

Essential to keep in mind is that in social justice (cultural Marxism), oppression by the majority is not tyrannically imposed oppression, something done by force. Instead, it exists in the common-sense ideas of liberal culture, which in America includes concepts taught in Christianity. This may include things such as objectivity, a strong work ethic, personal responsibility, meritocracy, and understanding the family to be composed of monogamous heterosexual marriage with children unless providentially hindered.

Antonio Francesco Gramsci was a significant Italian Marxist philosopher.[10] He is considered a key neo-Marxist. Both Marx and Gramsci grappled with the question of why the proletariat (workers) did not rise

---

position of cultural Marxism.

10. Antonio Francesco Gramsci, January 22, 1891–April 27, 1937

in rebellion against the bourgeoisie (the people with capital, businesses, or land). Although there are various components in the failure of Marxism, we can say not enough of the proletariat bought into his theory, and they actually adopted the standards of the bourgeoisie, which created the middle class.[11]

Gramsci's theory is called *cultural hegemony* (hegemony means predominance or domination), which is the domination by one group over other groups in society. Cultural hegemony contends that rather than using violence or force to maintain the bourgeoisie's dominance (majority's oppression), the dominant ruling class oppresses by making their values the common-sense and accepted norm of the culture. That is, the dominant group promotes its values as true, natural, and inevitable.

Applying Gramsci's cultural hegemony to America would seem to provide two primary responses to this hegemony (predominance of the majority white culture) that perpetuate the standards of the majority, the status quo. One, the oppressed believe the norms of the dominant group, such as meritocracy, are natural and adopt them. They conclude they remain oppressed because they do not deserve to have more. After all, they are neither as accomplished nor contribute as much to society as their oppressors. If this group is awakened (becomes woke) to their oppressed state being the result of artificial socially constructed norms, the revolution can begin; otherwise, they continue to accept their impoverished condition.

Two, some of the oppressed adopt the norms of the majority and take advantage of them and succeed. They prosper in society just as those who are in the dominant group. Both responses are considered wrong because they are built on the hegemonic idea that the dominant group's values are natural and inevitable when they are actually, according to Gramsci, a social construct that needs to be resisted, overthrown, and replaced with a natural and equitable system such as socialism or communism.[12]

Understanding this dynamic helps to shed light on the victim culture in America, which derives its validity and vitality from promoting its victimhood as being the result of a social construct hegemony rather than a natural and moral one. To wit, they are victims of an unnatural and biased

---

11. There are other theories why the revolution did not happen.

12. Of course, Gramsci notwithstanding, the acceptance of a set of norms need not be *proven* to be natural or inevitable to be legitimate. The only thing needed is that they can be demonstrated to be the morally superior and economically best for the highest number of citizens and the country as a whole; for a Christian, this would mean a set of norms that are consistent with and reflective of biblical teaching and principles.

4

set of norms. This victimhood is also the mentality that results in the ones who adopt victim status, rejecting those from their group who succeed and thrive under the dominant cultural system, which results in them being called Uncle Tom or said to be acting white. People like Condoleezza Rice, Clarence Thomas, Ben Carson, and Thomas Sowell serve as stellar examples of successful blacks being called Uncle Tom. Additionally, there are countless black people who equal or surpass their white counterparts all across America who receive the same disrespect from the victim culture.

Because rather than adopting a correct set of values (rights and wrongs), they are said to have adopted the white man's standards, which are unnatural and oppressive; therefore, they are not really black. Essential to keep in mind is that social justice's use of black and white includes more than skin color, although that is a part of what being black or white means. Being black or white consists of a mindset, a cultural identity.

Accordingly, blacks who succeed have become white, thereby perpetuating the majority's artificial domination. The oppressed group that does not thrive must reject those from their group who succeed in order to sustain the narrative of their victimhood and that the present system is systemically unjust—racist. The rejection of those blacks who succeed must happen in order to maintain the viability of the claim of being a victim, which is essential for fueling the necessary revolution that will overthrow the present capitalistic (and in the case of the USA, Christian) system of values. People like Jesse Jackson and Al Sharpton exist to promote and by promoting victimhood.

The revolution, through protests, riots, and anarchy, supposedly will usher in a just system of socialism and communism (equal outcomes for all groups regardless of whether or not everyone exercises personal responsibility). If the oppressed group that rejects the dominant morals and standards did not discredit the successful blacks, who liberate themselves from being oppressed and succeed by exercising personal responsibility and adopting the standards of the dominant culture, the claim of victimhood could not survive. Because the mere acknowledgment that black people can rise out of their lowly estate and remain black discredits the essential claim of victimhood and systemic and structural racism.

Thus, the *actual* failure on the part of the supposedly oppressed is that, in America, they see the path to success as forsaking their blackness and becoming white rather than seeing themselves as Americans adopting the American path to success—something all people have to do to succeed in

America regardless of their race. We should all note that Gramsci does the same thing he accuses the capitalist of doing; he promotes his socialism and communism as natural.

Here is the biblical response: biblically, anyone can be a racist or commit any other sin that humans can commit and then be forgiven and given a new life (John 3:1–4; Rom 10:9–19). Racism is not determined by one's past, group size, or skin color, but by their heart, as reflected in their actions (Matt 15:18–20). For example, murder and adultery are sinful desires of the heart even if there is no physical murder or adultery (Mark 7:21; Matt 5:27–32).

All are privileged in some way over other people. All people have some opportunities that others do not. Privilege does not equal oppression or make a person an oppressor. Having less privilege or opportunity does not necessarily mean a person or group is oppressed by the ones who have more. Abraham was wealthy (Gen 24:35), Israel was privileged in being God's chosen nation (Rom 3:1–2), and Paul was privileged as a Roman citizen (Acts 16:37–38; 22:28).[13] Thus, everyone experiences privilege in comparison to someone else. Privilege is not a sin, and therefore does not require a sense of guilt or repentance; it requires only faithfulness and good stewardship.

Opportunities (privilege) can be accepted and require only that the recipients be faithful as good stewards of the opportunity, which involve being thankful (Eph 5:20). That is the theme of the parable of the talents (Matt 25:14–30). The one who was given more talents did not have to repent of privilege, nor were the ones who received fewer considered victims. They were judged only on whether they were faithful stewards of what they had. This same truth is evident when the Jews were slaves in Egypt and the Babylonian captivity (Exodus and Daniel, respectively).

Additionally, this parable, as well as history and the rest of Scripture, demonstrates that opportunity or privilege does not equal achievement. Many are given privileges or opportunities only to squander them. Privilege grants an opportunity for development, but it does not grant success. Achievement comes about by capitalizing on the opportunity. We also know that while we can give someone an opportunity, we cannot guarantee a probability of success because the opportunity is not the agent for success;

---

13. Jews were also privileged in that salvation was of the Jew first, Rom 1:16, they were God's chosen (his) people (Rom 11:1), custodians of God's word (Rom 3:2), and the people through whom Christ came (Rom 9:5), "Salvation is from the Jews" (John 4:22). In Paul's ministry he sought out the Jews first in every new city (Acts 13:5, 14; 14:1; 17:2, 10, 17; 18:4, 19; 19:8).

that belongs to the individual. For example, we can give someone the chance to get an education or experience salvation through hearing the gospel. Still, we cannot guarantee they will be a good steward of that opportunity.

The most significant privilege and call to stewardship and faithfulness is the call to receive the gospel unto salvation (Prov 10:5; Ps 95:6–8; Isa 55:6; John 12:35–36; 2 Cor 6:2). In eternity, what the individual did with that opportunity will matter more than all others combined. Every person who hears the gospel is more privileged than if he were a billionaire and did not hear, although I believe every person hears the gospel.[14] Therefore, praise and thanksgiving should flow from every life who hears the gospel.

It should be noted that the very nature of social justice, critical race theory, and intersectionality are to divide. They divide individuals, groups, and even Christians. Christians who advocate any of these are dividing non-Christians as well as Christians. Creating such divisions is antithetical to the gospel and Christianity (Eph 4:4–7). Rather than confronting individuals with their own sin and need of repentance lest they die and perish in hell (Luke 5:32; 13:3; Rev 22:7–8), cultural Marxism and intersectionality provide an excuse to blame other people.

---

14. See my book *Does God Love All or Some?*

2

Understanding the Nature of the Conflict

THIS BOOK WILL EXAMINE cultural Marxism and social justice, along with their various components, through the lens of Scripture. I will contrast the biblical perspective with that of social justice and highlight how social justice undermines biblical truth and corrupts the gospel of Jesus Christ.

The theories I will discuss have been taught in academia for decades. They are the basis of identity politics in the Democratic Party. Now we must face their presence in conservative, evangelical Christianity and the SBC. I do believe genuine racism exists, but I do not think critical theory, cultural Marxism, critical race theory, intersectionality, and social justice are descriptive or reflective of actual racism.[1] Critical race theory asserts that race is not grounded in biology but is a social construct created by white people to oppress black people; consequently, whites are racists, and blacks are not. Therefore, social justice concepts do not accurately explain the nature of actual racism, nor can they offer an adequate remedy for real racism. Genuine racism is the belief that one or more ethnicities or races are inherently inferior. Since the inferiority is innate, it cannot be overcome. Or it can be turned around where one ethnicity or race believes their race is inherently superior to others. Accordingly, anyone can be racist. This contrast in meaning should serve as a reminder that before we discuss racism, we need to define the term.

1. The term "intersectionality" was coined in 1989 by Kimberlé Crenshaw, a black, full-time professor at the UCLA School of Law and Columbia Law School. She is an American lawyer, civil rights advocate, and a leading scholar of critical race theory. She used it to demonstrate that social justice happens at multiple levels. Perlman, "Origin of 'Intersectionality.'"

The origin of critical theory is a think tank called the Institute for Social Research at the Frankfurt School in Germany, which eventually became known as the Frankfurt School.[2] The expected Utopia that was supposed to arise from classical Marxism never appeared.[3] Critical theory arose to correct the deficiencies of classical Marxism and, therefore, bring about a just society.[4] What sets critical theory apart from other social theories is social theories generally seek to *explain* society, whereas critical theory aims to *change* society. This change entails deconstructing the existing culture and ushering in a more just society, which means a socialistic or communistic society. In critical theory, there is the assumption of oppressors and oppression.

In 1933, Hitler rose to power, and he viewed Marxism as an enemy, which resulted in several pivotal thinkers of the Frankfurt School fleeing to New York. There, they took teaching positions at Columbia University. Stephen Thomas Kirschner says, "The Frankfurt School was loosely reestablished at Columbia, this time focusing on American society, rather than German."[5] After the fall of the Third Reich, all but Herbert Marcuse left their teaching positions at Columbia and returned to Germany. It was Marcuse who established what we know as cultural Marxism.

Kirschner says, "In the 1950s, Marcuse stated the Marxist revolution would not be brought about by 'the proletariat' but by a coalition of blacks, feminist women, homosexuals, and students. This is where the term

---

2. There is a sense in which Karl Marx was the first critical theorist, at least in modern times, since he evaluated society to change it, and his evaluation was composed of oppressors and the oppressed.

3. Stephen Thomas Kirschner says, "Marx believed that feudalism would lead to capitalism. Capitalism would create massive inequality between the rich and the poor. The workers would all rise up and overthrow the hated 'bourgeoisie' (the upper class). There would then be a 'dictatorship of the proletariat' (the workers) which would ensure equality. Then that government would wear away and break down, and the world would be left with this utopian, egalitarian society. (Although, how and why government would break down and equality would be ensured was never clearly explained.)" Kirschner, "Cultural Marxism," para. 3.

4. Kirschner says, "In 1937, [Max] Horkheimer wrote about what is today known as 'critical theory.' Critical theory is a social theory which is about criticizing the way a culture and 'society as a whole' function, in order to change it. Contrast this with other social theories, which are more just about understanding and interpreting why things are as they are." Kirschner, "Cultural Marxism," paras. 20–22.

5. Kirschner, "Cultural Marxism," para. 19.

'Cultural Marxism' comes from, as it is applied to marginalized groups rather than class."[6]

Similar to classical Marxism, there must be a clash between groups. In cultural Marxism, it is the oppressors (majorities) and the oppressed (minorities). Critical theory is the source of cultural Marxism, and cultural Marxism is the advocacy and application of critical theory. Critical race theory and intersectionality are components of critical theory and cultural Marxism.[7] Presently, social justice is the most common term used in America to express the essence of cultural Marxism.

Consequently, when you hear the term social justice, you should think of critical theory, cultural Marxism, critical race theory, and intersectionality. You should not think justice as understood to mean equality before the law or even equality of opportunity; by equality, social justice advocates mean equal outcomes—socialism. Thomas Sowell, Senior Fellow at the Hoover Institute, asks, "How does one explain the *origins* of something like inequality, which has been ubiquitous as far back as recorded history goes?"[8] His book demonstrates multiple factors that result in unequal outcomes rather than simplistically reducing inequality to one cause, such as social injustice—cultural Marxism. This is true whether one is considering a particular country or the world. Thus, he says, "The probability that all of these combinations and permutations would work out in such a way as to produce even approximately equal economic outcomes around the world is remote."[9]

6. Kirschner, "Cultural Marxism," para. 29.

7. "Critical Theory has a narrow and a broad meaning in philosophy and in the history of the social sciences. 'Critical Theory' in the narrow sense designates several generations of German philosophers and social theorists in the Western European Marxist tradition known as the Frankfurt School. According to these theorists, a 'critical' theory may be distinguished from a 'traditional' theory according to a specific practical purpose: a theory is critical to the extent that it seeks human 'emancipation from slavery,' acts as a 'liberating . . . influence,' and works 'to create a world which satisfies the needs and powers' of human beings (Max Horkheimer 1972, 246). Because such theories aim to explain and transform all the circumstances that enslave human beings, many 'critical theories' in the broader sense have been developed. They have emerged in connection with the many social movements that identify varied dimensions of the domination of human beings in modern societies. In both the broad and the narrow senses, however, a critical theory provides the descriptive and normative bases for social inquiry aimed at decreasing domination and increasing freedom in all their forms." Bohman, "Critical Theory," para. 1.

8. Sowell, *Wealth, Poverty, and Politics*, 2.

9. Sowell, *Wealth, Poverty, and Politics*, 20.

Nevertheless, social justice reduces the cause of unequal outcomes to social injustice, which Marxism is supposed to be able to cure even though it has never done so. Additionally, you should never equate social justice with God's justice, as revealed in Scripture, because social justice is based on materialistic Marxism, and, therefore, is in fundamental opposition to biblical justice.

Cultural Marxism consists of an extensive, complex, and fundamentally different set of ideas, individuals, groups, and diverse approaches. I believe this fact alone significantly contributes to the high level of difficulty associated with understanding and identifying cultural Marxism. Dr. E. S. Williams's insight is helpful to see how all of these fundamentally dissimilar ideas fit together. He teaches that common to all of these ideas "is the creation of interdisciplinary theories that might serve as instruments of social transformation."[10] This association can include concepts such as social justice, feminism, and neo-progressivism, which are all "inspired by or born out of critical theory."[11]

Dr. Williams also remarks that in cultural Marxism, "Every aspect of a person's identity is to be questioned, every norm or standard in society challenged and ideally altered in order to benefit supposedly oppressed groups."[12] The identity aspects can include such things as family, religion, and government. Dr. Williams further says, "Key points of critical race theory: 1) Institutional racism is pervasive; 2) People of color are oppressed by white privilege and white supremacy."[13] Consider the following in order to understand the way social justice seeks to transform society. Think of how we have defined such common ideas as family, marriage, the individual, education, sin, racism, oppression, oppressed, government, freedom, responsibility, justice, God, and even the gospel, and realize that social justice redefines such terms so that they are inherently different and unrecognizable to the average Christian or citizen. The Christian who does not understand this transformation of meaning in such common terms often falls prey to adopting some of the new ideas hidden within the old terms.

This is the definition of the Encyclopedia Britannica: "Critical theory: Marxist-inspired movement in social and political philosophy originally associated with the work of the Frankfurt School. Drawing particularly

10. Thenewcalvinist, "Stain," 8:08–14.
11. Thenewcalvinist, "Stain," 8:37–47.
12. Thenewcalvinist, "Stain," 8:58–9:09.
13. Thenewcalvinist, "Stain," 13:00–13:14.

on the thought of Karl Marx and Sigmund Freud, critical theorists maintain that a primary goal of the philosophy is to understand and to help overcome the social structures through which people are dominated and oppressed."[14] It is crucial to keep in mind that Marx, Freud, and other key players like Friedrich Engels were all materialists. They denied God, the soul and spirit of man, and the entire immaterial world, which makes them in absolute opposition to Christianity. Critical theory's materialistic foundations highlight the unacceptableness of Resolution 9 that was adopted at the 2019 Southern Baptist Convention, which endorsed critical race theory and intersectionality as reliable analytical tools (see chapter 9 and appendices 2, 3, and 4).

Social justice is accomplished by favoring one group (the oppressed/minority/non-sinners) and punishing the other group (the oppressors/majority/sinners) by redistribution of wealth and power. Civil measures may accomplish redistribution, but most likely, it will take a revolution and forced redistribution of wealth and power. The Communist Manifesto states, "The Communists disdain to conceal their views and aims. They openly declare that their ends can be attained only by the forcible overthrow of all existing social conditions. Let the ruling classes tremble at a Communistic revolution."[15]

As in Marxism, social justice emphasizes group identity and responsibility rather than individual identity and responsibility. The groups may be composed of people who neither suffered nor inflicted wrong. Merit or guilt is based on such things as skin color or sex. Social justice determines what is right and wrong and what the penalties and corrections should be; these may be antithetical to true biblical justice. What social justice calls justice is, at times, categorically condemned in Scripture as sin. For example, the oppressed are minorities, which include homosexuals and transgender people. These groups are viewed as normal and good while being white and heterosexual makes someone an oppressor—abnormal and bad. And heterosexuality is not morally better than homosexuality or being transgender. Cultural Marxism, with its identity politics, divides rather than unites.

14. The article goes on to say, "Believing that science, like other forms of knowledge, has been used as an instrument of oppression, they caution against a blind faith in scientific progress, arguing that scientific knowledge must not be pursued as an end in itself without reference to the goal of human emancipation. Since the 1970s, critical theory has been immensely influential in the study of history, law, literature, and the social sciences." See "Critical Theory."

15. Marx and Engels, "Position of the Communists," para. 11.

As an American, people should be judged on such things as their character, contribution to the company or society, or academic achievement for acceptance into a school. This is reflective of meritocracy, personal responsibility, and the Christian work ethic (2 Thess 3:10). Identity politics destroys this model. Identity politics focuses on group identity (race, sex, minority status) as being sufficient to make a person rewardable even if he does not contribute to the task at hand or meet the same qualifications that others have to meet to enjoy the same opportunity. Accordingly, if a person belongs to an oppressed group (minority), they deserve preference for that fact alone (affirmative action and diversity quotas), which takes us back to judging people based on the color of their skin rather than as Martin Luther King said, "the content of their character."[16]

A person's identity is determined by what group a person belongs to, and it is deepened by how many intersecting layers of discrimination the person believes she has experienced. The person may identify as a black lesbian, as a transgender person, or any number of social identities that contribute to the type of systemic discrimination the individual believes she has experienced. Social justice, cultural Marxism, intersectionality, and identity politics divide people into postmodern Marxian groups based on our differences. Since there is no unifying, absolute, standard set of values, acknowledgment of knowable truth, or even objective meaning of words in a postmodern Marxian paradigm, we cannot even identify what it means to be an American. If we proclaim specific standards, we are called oppressors and racists because there are no true or even superior norms according to postmodernism; there are just relative multicultural norms.

We can see this postmodern Marxism in the destruction of every previous unifying and agreed-upon idea (such as religion, history, personal responsibility, hard work, family, education, morality, structure, monuments, and anthems) that we as Americans unified around; they helped to depict what it meant to be an American.[17] Such destruction of all unifying qualities of America is nowhere more graphically displayed than in the unwillingness to stand at the National Anthem or Pledge of Allegiance, and the willingness to burn the flag, which is the most significant symbol of these *United* States. All this leaves us with is 'states' in America, but little if

16. King, "I Have a Dream," para. 20.

17. Postmodernism began as a literary and artistic movement that rejected the dogmas and principles of modernism, or any other set of doctrines or absolutes. It now encompasses a full-life perspective of rejecting knowable objective standards—including Christian absolutes.

13

anything to unify around; hence, the fall of America. Moreover, these inter-sectionally-divided groups cannot even civilly and effectively communicate with each other. Because, based on intersectionality, only the minority or oppressed groups can even know the truth, and based on postmodernism, words have no objective meaning (we cannot know the authorial intent), only subjective meaning; that is, what they mean to the hearer.

In contrast, biblically, all people are created in the image of God, and, therefore, belong to the human race and are essentially equal. We, as hu-mans, are all sinful by choice and deserve judgment. Our injustices are first and foremost against God's holiness and his holy law. Consequently, we are all equally in need of redemption. Because God loves us, Christ paid for the sins of the world so that every person can be saved, which is God's desire. Accordingly, our identity in creation is in that we are all a part of the human race, created in the image of God and sinful by nature and choice. Spiritually, those that accept God's love and payment for their sins by faith in Christ and his sacrifice become Christians, which is our identity. The social justice perspective with its identity politics divides, whereas the bibli-cal perspective unifies.

The cultural Marxism grid can transform virtually any biblical im-morality into morality as long as a minority of the people practice the sin. Because minority status equals being the oppressed group (which is the righteous group to belong to), that makes the majority who believe the act is a sin to be the evil oppressors. Thus, the biblical sin is sanitized by the dominant Marxian sin of oppression. Therefore, those whose lifestyles include biblical sin are normalized and protected. Presently this includes groups such as homosexuals and transgenders. It seems very likely that in the future, it will consist of people who practice pedophilia and bestiality, as well as a host of other unthinkable vile debaucheries. California's legis-lature has already passed a bill that provides greater leniency toward those who have homosexual sex with a minor. The bill has been sent to Governor Gavin Newsom.[18]

The recognition of the presence of cultural Marxism and social justice does not require that some injustices they stand against are not real injus-tices. Even those who are not social justice advocates may agree with social justice advocates on some injustices. The methods used by social justice advocates may differ dramatically from ordinary citizens who believe a

18. Governor Newsom signed the bill into law on September 11, 2020. Koseff, "New-som Signs Bill."

Need to distinguish b/t legitimate sins (homosexuality) and ethnicity

14

wrong has been committed and needs to be made right. Some social justice advocates may use riots, destruction of private property, and even killing innocent people, which was foreshadowed by their Marxian predecessors who did the same in the riots of the sixties.[19] The elites who support the concept of social justice but are not on the streets rioting make their voices heard through the media, public speaking, writing, and academia.[20] They, too, seek the dismantling of the present capitalistic civil system of America as necessary to usher in a socialistic Utopia.

The people who are not social justice warriors, but who also see the injustice and reject rioting, will often peaceably protest and work through the justice system and legislative and elective processes. Additionally, to refer to an event as being influenced or caused by cultural Marxism or social justice does not mean everyone involved is a social justice warrior. Nor does it mean that everyone embraces every aspect of cultural Marxism any more than to say everyone at the rally was a Christian means everyone accepts every Baptist doctrine. It only means that cultural Marxists are either leading the charge or heavily involved in various ways.

Consequently, exposing the Marxist presence and influence in a cultural conflict is not equivalent to being dismissive of an actual injustice, nor does it signify indifference to the presence of other motivators for some who are involved. This is a charge that is often made when we speak of the influence of cultural Marxism, but it is a baseless charge.

To avoid confusion, remember that regardless of which specific area we are considering, critical theory, cultural Marxism, critical race theory, intersectionality, or social justice, we are discussing the philosophy of materialistic Marxism, which is antithetical to God, Christianity, Scripture, and God's justice. In each of the following sections, I will contrast elements of cultural Marxism with the relevant biblical truth. As mentioned, I will frequently use social justice interchangeably with cultural Marxism since, generally speaking, they seek the same things and utilize similar methods. While social justice may not entail every aspect of cultural Marxism, they are very similar in that both employ anarchist measures in their strategy and favor socialism or communism over capitalism. They also define justice contrary to true biblical justice, favor redistribution of wealth and power by force, and seek a socialistic Utopia.

19. Gorkin, "How the 1960s Riots Foreshadow."
20. Chamberlain, "Riots Break Out."

3

Race, Cultural Marxism, and Classical Marxism

The Differences

THIS CHAPTER WILL BEGIN by contrasting cultural Marxism's understanding of race with biblical teaching. Then I will compare classical Marxism with cultural Marxism.

Race Defined by Critical Race Theory

The Encyclopedia Britannica defines critical race theory thusly as "the view that the law and legal institutions are inherently racist and that race itself, instead of being biologically grounded and natural, is a socially constructed concept that is used by white people to further their economic and political interests at the expense of people of colour."[1] Critical race theory's perspective makes race merely a social construct to promote white supremacy. Critical race theory makes racism (white supremacy and privilege) present in *every* interracial interaction and relationship. Therefore, the question,

---

1. Curry, "Critical Race Theory," para. 1. In between the time when I originally cited this entry and the time of this book's publication, the Encyclopedia Britannica's definition of the term "critical race theory" evidently changed, providing an interesting insight into the terminological fluidity regarding our time and this subject. Here is the original: "Race, instead of being biologically grounded and natural, is socially constructed; and that race as a socially constructed concept functions as a means to maintain the interests of the white population that constructed it."

according to critical race theory, is not *is* racism present, but instead, the question is, *how* is racism present in this situation. Importantly, cultural Marxism, like classical Marxism, espouses a materialistic view of humans and divides humans rather than uniting them. This view, as I will demonstrate, is the opposite of Scripture.

Race Defined Biblically

All people belong to the human race, and therefore, all are equal, being created in the image of God (Gen 1:26–28). God later created multiple languages and dispersed the people into different geographical locations (Gen 11:7–9). Out of this scattered, geographically diverse, and multilingual human race developed different biologically common traits for the various groups, more languages and dialects, and subcultures, which became known as ethnicities, nationalities, and races. These are often associated with language, skin color, and geographical origin. Accordingly, all races and ethnicities are understood in the sense of Gen 1:26–28, Gen 11:7–9, and other biblical distinctions such as tribe, people, tongue, and nation (Rev 7:9; 11:9). We may, therefore, note five essentials that unite all human beings.

1. All people belong to the human race (Gen 1:26–28).

2. All people are created in the image of God (Gen 1:26–28).

3. All people are fallen in sin (Gen 3).

4. Christ salvationally loves and died for all people (John 3:16).

5. The saved are reconciled to God and each other and forgiven of *all* their sins (Rom 8:1; Eph 2:10–20).

Race defined biblically necessarily rejects *actual* racism. Merriam-Webster Dictionary defines racism as: "A belief that race is the primary determinant of human traits and capacities and that racial differences produce an *inherent superiority* of a particular race"[2] (italics added). Genuine

2. See Merriam-Webster's definition of "racism." Defined by Cambridge Dictionary, racism is "policies, behaviors, rules, etc. that result in a continued unfair advantage to some people and unfair or harmful treatment of others based on race: harmful or unfair things that people say, do, or think based on the belief that their own race makes them more intelligent, good, moral, etc. than people of other races." "Racism," para. 1. Similar to the Encyclopedia Britannica update in the previous footnote, the definition from Cambridge Dictionary was changed at some point. Here is the original: "the belief that

racism is the sin of partiality, which is condemned in Scripture (Lev 19:15; Jas 2:1–9; 3:13–18). Accordingly, the biblical perspective of race necessarily rejects race as defined by critical race theory or as popularly used in American culture, which reduces it to a weapon to divide and silence anyone who disagrees with liberal or socialistic policies.

Classical Marxism Defined

Classical Marxism proposes a clash between the proletariat (the working class) and the bourgeoisie (property and business owners). The problem to be resolved is the elimination of economic oppression. The fundamental evil in the world is the oppression of workers by those who have capital—capitalism. It is the tension that arises from the *haves* subjugating the *have nots*. In Marxism, the haves or "sinners" are keeping Utopia from arriving, but the have nots are free from the sin of the haves or anything else that stands in the way of bringing in Utopia. The have nots cannot be oppressors in the Marxist sense. Therefore, the haves need to repent but cannot, so long as they are the haves, and the have nots need no repentance.

The solution is to eliminate the free market, capitalism, and private property through the expansion of state ownership by taxation or even confiscation of the capital of the bourgeoisie. This resolution permits the state to redistribute the wealth of the bourgeoisie to the proletariat so that all people (both groups) are equal; equal means all experience equal outcomes regardless of such things as personal merit or work ethic. The acquisition of wealth from the bourgeoisie can be accomplished through such devices as graduated income tax or outright seizure through anarchy or other means so that the just society (Utopia) can begin. But Marxism failed to produce the promised Utopia. Moreover, it can never create a just society because it is based on a fatally flawed, materialistic view of man and his world, reality.

Classical and cultural Marxism promote the idea that either you cannot, or it is highly improbable that you will, usher in the Utopic state with consensual democratic politics. Marxists contend that the problem is systemic. Consequently, every structure, whether it is religious, legal, business, familial, or available opportunity, is inherently corrupt. Therefore, everything, including all structures of norms, order, and authority,

---

people's qualities are influenced by their race and that the members of other races are not as good as the members of your own, or the resulting unfair treatment of members of other races."

must be critiqued (destroyed) and ultimately replaced, which will usher in Utopia. Understanding this aspect of Marxism will help you make sense out of the violence and anarchical behavior by some in their quest to bring about change, which is also either excused or minimized by many who do not physically participate in the anarchy. Although the accusation of systemic racism is everywhere, we should not accept its reality as a given. It is up to those who charge its presence to prove it exists. Speaking of events in the past or anecdotally does not confirm systemic racism. The claim of systemic and structural racism throughout the very fiber of America is severely undermined by the millions of successful blacks and black-owned businesses. I reject the idea that America is systemically racist, or as some say, racism is in our DNA, thereby signifying that America is pervasively a racist country.[3] In truth, there may be no other country in the world that has done more to correct the unjustness of racism than America except for Great Britain. Notably, it is only the Western hemisphere, heavily influenced by Christianity, that later developed a moral consciousness against slavery; ultimately, leading to the end of slavery in most of the world.

Biblical Evaluation of Marxism

Biblically, the problem is sin. Scripture is clear that all humans are infected with and purveyors of sin (Rom 3:10–18). The solution for all humanity's ills is found in trusting Christ as Savior, which God desires everyone to do (John 3:16). God responds by making the repentant into a new creation (John 3:1–4, 16; 2 Cor 5:17), and the redeemed are to walk according to his word (1 John 5:3) and by the power of his Spirit (Eph 5:18).[4] If all humans in society lived according to God's word and his strength, we would experience the justest society possible in a fallen world, which will be surpassed only in the new world where sin is no more (Rev 21).

---

3. Sometimes, systemic and structural racism are used interchangeably to refer to processes or procedures that disadvantage blacks. Institutional racism is sometimes used to speak of things that block black people from accessing services, goods, and opportunities of society. Regularly, all three are used interchangeably, which is the way I use them in this book.

4. I use repentance and faith as two aspects of the same act. Repentance is, by God's grace, turning from sin, and faith is turning to Christ. In other words, true forgiveness does not leave us where or what we were. We embrace Christ and abandon who we were; therefore, we turn from something, our sin, to someone, Christ. The turning in repentance is in the mind, which is evidenced by commensurate following actions.

The biblical picture is the opposite of classical Marxism because Scripture confirms creation, whereas classical Marxism believes in materialism. Consequently, Marxism does not recognize the real source of man's problems, which is sin, nor does it know the real source of help, which is God and salvation. Therefore, Marxist analysis and liberation are irreparably flawed. Biblically, sin is defined as a breach of God's holy standard and is against God first, rather than wrong being defined as the oppression of the working class. It is not a political revolution that ushers in the Utopia. It is the King of Kings ushering in his righteous kingdom (Rev 21).

Cultural Marxism Defined

Cultural Marxism proposes a clash between the oppressed (minorities) and the oppressor (majority). The problem is that the "majority groups are typically defined as privileged and oppressive, with minority groups accordingly labeled underprivileged and oppressed."[5] In the USA and most of Europe, this means that white people are the oppressors, white supremacists, and the oppressed are black people. But the paradigm is broad enough to include other minorities as well.

Because the problem is systemic, the solution is the redistribution of wealth and power by challenging and dismantling (critiquing) all structures of the current society. The majority (oppressors) must be punished and are seen as the evil source of oppression. Majorities can include such groups as white people, Christians, and heterosexuals, but predominately it is directed toward white people. The oppressors must be repudiated, and their power and privilege transferred to the minorities (oppressed), and the result will be a just society. This change may come about through peaceful means such as changing laws, norms, and elections as well as graduated taxation, but it probably will not. Consequently, there will need to be the seizure of wealth and power by other means such as anarchy or a revolution; this will ultimately result in a new government of socialism. The use of anarchist tactics serves several purposes, one of which is to demonstrate that American capitalism is a failed system that needs to be replaced with socialism.

Significantly, whether through taxation, revolution, or mixing capitalism with socialism as Stalin did, socialism relies on others creating the wealth for it to manage. We can trace this pattern to Marx himself. Some

5. Thenewcalvinist, "Stain," 9:36–44.

of Marx's contemporaries characterized his relationships with other people as self-serving. For example, while Marx did work at various jobs, he lived primarily off of others. First, he lived off his father, who was a lawyer, Baron and capitalist. After his father died, Marx lived off his mother's inheritance until she cut him off. Later he continued his upper-class lifestyle with continued financial help from Friedrich Engels, who worked for his capitalist father's company.

Marx always lived beyond his means at the expense of others. This lifestyle eventually resulted in him, his wife, and children (his wife came out of the aristocracy) living in squalor for twenty years. Even then, he continued spending more than he had and refused to live in proletariat housing. His three daughters also married men who could not support them. Fortunately, Engels also provided considerable help to them from the resources he obtained while working for his capitalist father.[6] Marx's life was a great illustration of the former prime minister of England Margaret Thatcher's summary of socialism when she said, "Socialist governments traditionally do make a financial mess. They always run out of other people's money."[7]

Privilege, "white privilege," includes the idea of white supremacy of all white people, and all white people should feel guilty and repent of living privileged lives. But they cannot remove the stain of living racist, privileged lives or their guilt because they are white (white supremacists). According to cultural Marxism, white people are racists, white supremacists, even if they reject every form of real racism from a biblical perspective. Cultural Marxism is the source of identity politics, and critical race theory and intersectionality serve as the means of its promotion. Consequently, the left continually calls people racists because they base their understanding of racism on critical race theory or weaponized racism, neither of which are actual racism. James Lindsay summarizes the ubiquity of being called a racist well. He says, "Critical Race Theory proceeds upon a number of core tenets, the first and most central of which is that racism is the ordinary state of affairs in our society. It is not aberrational, and therefore it is assumed to be present in all phenomena and interactions."[8]

6. Sowell, "Marx the Man."

7. Gardner, "Thames TV This Week," para. 78. This is popularly known as "The trouble with socialism is that eventually, you run out of other people's money," Thatcher, "Margaret Thatcher," para. 4.

8. Lindsay, "For Racial Healing," para. 4.

A Corruption of Consequence

Truth claims by the oppressors are always suspect. In contrast, truth claims made by the oppressed are always credible until proven false, which intersectionality makes almost impossible since the privileged oppressors do not understand the real truth. This philosophy turns innocent until proven guilty on its head. It also exchanges individual identity and responsibility (Christianity) for group identity and responsibility (Marxism). This exchange is true whether we are referring to classical or cultural Marxism. If you belong to the majority, you are an oppressor by that fact alone.

This is also where standpoint epistemology weighs in. Epistemology is the study of what we can know and how we can know. Standpoint epistemology stresses that a person's ability to know is always socially situated. Resultantly, a person can only know based on their experience in society as an oppressor or an oppressed. However, only the oppressed can know reality or objective truth. The oppressor is blinded from the truth of reality by his privileged societal position. While some talk as though there is no objective truth, it is necessary to understand that some critical theorists say there is objective truth, but the oppressed are the only ones in a position to know the actual truth; the oppressor cannot. Even truth claims made by the majority are seen as oppressive. Here again, we find social justice in absolute opposition to Christianity, wherein the Scripture is the truth (John 17:17) and judge of all truth claims, and anyone can know the truth (John 8:32; 19:35; 20:30–31) and the one who is the Truth (John 14:6)!

Virtually everything in postmodern social justice is seen as the conflict and result of power. It is all about power. The success that anyone achieves is attributed to the power they have. That is why social justice is not just about opportunity, equality before the law, or wealth, but the redistribution of power. Little if anything is acknowledged to come about through hard work and competency. They view accomplishment and success as the product of power. Whoever has the power will have success.

While it may be that some who succeed have power, success cannot be reduced to that. People succeed because they contribute to society by offering products or services for which others are willing to pay. For example, plumbers do not make money because of power, but because of hard work and using their skills and competency in a way that benefit others. People see paying for their help to be more beneficial than keeping the money that it costs them. Postmodern cultural Marxism reduces everything to power except when they need help (such as a plumber, doctor, accountant). Then they choose the most skilled person they can find; thus, the hypocrisy of postmodern social justice is exposed. Like all of us, the wildest postmodern Marxist wants the most competent pilot flying the plane he is on and not the most powerful; he hopes his pilot was not chosen based on power.

Contrary to cultural Marxism, differences in opportunities and outcomes can be due to a variety of things such as personal irresponsibility or responsibility, family dynamics, socially inherited attitudes, work ethic, geographical location, physical ability, cultural value system, and intellectual or physical ability. Also, there can be non-racist systemic conditions such as a cultural breakdown of the family, rampant crime, lack of emphasis on education, no good educational options, and devaluing those who break out of a broken family or a limiting culture while making heroes out of drug lords and criminals.

For example, many blacks who should be viewed by black people as role models, such as Justice Clarence Thomas, Ben Carson, Condoleezza Rice, Larry Elder, and countless others, say they are called Uncle Tom, coon, or told that they are not even black by other black people. Candace Owens says since becoming a conservative, as a black person, she has been called a white supremacist. Blacks who seek to be successful in education, career, and life are often derogatorily described as trying to be white. Thomas Sowell says, "All across the country, there are heartbreaking stories about young blacks in schools who condemn those among them who try to be good students as 'acting white.'"[9] Conservative blacks tell of simple things like punctuality, striving for good grades, doing homework, and speaking proper English that will bring the charge of "acting white."

Actually, that is acting American. In America, much privilege is tied to hard work and economics, which all Americans can aspire to without selling out their heritage. Some of these same black people elevate the status of some of the most violent rappers, wronged criminals, and Ebonics. Successful blacks who learned the English of the culture (as every immigrant and white person has to do to succeed) are said to have sold out to the white man. Even though in any culture, not just America, everyone has to integrate with the dominant culture regarding language and work ethic to succeed—this does not include all their immoralities. Thus, if a person sees unequal outcomes as the sure proof of systemic racism, he either is a Marxist or has adopted Marxist thinking.

Given the reality that unequal outcomes do not demonstrate sure proof of racism, we can know that unequal outcomes do not necessarily

9. Sowell, *Controversial Essays*, 82.

make the one who has more the oppressor and the one who has less the oppressed.[10] To assert that unequal outcomes always demonstrate racism is to speak as a Marxist. We know that families and cultures that emphasize hard work, personal responsibility, education, and have both a mother and father in the home do better than those who do not. This is true whether it takes place in the home of a white or black family. We know that generally speaking, those who get an education, get a job, marry, and have children (in that order) do better than those who do not. This reality has nothing to do with racism, but the Marxists disagree.

The cultural Marxist argues that virtually every disparity of wealth and opportunity is the result of racism. They often do not even consider such things as personal responsibility, systemic fatherlessness, familial experiences and structures, the value placed on education, socially inherited attitudes, or geography.[11] To fail to recognize or give due consideration to other systemic hindrances and deterrents that are not racist is Marxian. This reality is true even if some do not like the label Marxist, which is not surprising given its history and the postmodern disdain of logical and descriptive language that the postmodern mind views as too limiting.

For example, Walter E. Williams was an American economist. He was the John M. Olin Distinguished Professor of Economics at George Mason University. He distinguishes between material poverty and behavior or spiritual poverty, saying, "The latter . . . refers to conduct and value that prevent the development of healthy families, a work ethic, and self-sufficiency. The absence of those values virtually guarantees pathological lifestyles that include drug and alcohol addiction, crime, violence, incarceration, illegitimacy, single-parent households, dependency, and erosion of the work ethic . . . For the most part, material poverty is no longer the problem it once was."[12] He continues to probe these topics on the following pages and throughout his book.[13] Here again, we are reminded of the fallacy of reducing the cause of black poverty (or any group living in a culture such as ours)

10. Even the birth order of children growing up in the same home results in significant differences in their level of success in certain areas, which cannot be due to racism.

11. See Walter E. Williams's argument that it is not racism or the legacy of slavery (victimhood) that is wreaking havoc in the black community. It is issues such as the decline of the black family, the lack of educational excellence, the high illegitimacy rate, the decline in marriage, the increase in divorce rates, and Great Society programs. Williams, *Liberty Versus Socialism*, 340–41, 354.

12. Williams, *Race & Economics*, 6.

13. Williams, *Race & Economics*, 6 and following.

to only one cause. To do so is a tragic and unjustified error that harms, and I believe, degrades black people.[14]

Some of the most impressive advances one can imagine have been made by black people even while in the shackles of slavery and the one hundred years following the end of slavery when many substantial impediments still stood in their way. These impediments were the precise result of actual injustices imposed on black people by white people. Their successes in some of the most challenging circumstances imaginable remind everyone they are created in the image of God.

Yet, as with cultural Marxism, progressivism blames the failure of minorities to succeed not on cultural or behavioral shortcomings but societal structure and racism. In academia, even the mention of cultural or familial values being the culprit can bring the wrath of the woke elite. Heather Mac Donald, Thomas W. Smith Fellow of the Manhattan Institute, says, "The founding idea of contemporary progressivism is that structural and individual racism lies behind socioeconomic inequalities. Discussing bad behavioral choices and maladaptive culture is out of bounds and will be punished mercilessly by slinging at the offender the usual fusillade of '-isms- (to be supplemented, post-Charlottesville, with frequent mentions of 'white supremacy')."[15] Additionally, this is a reminder that the ideas of cultural Marxism can be found under various leftwing labels, which does nothing to disassociate them from cultural Marxism.

Biblical Evaluation of Cultural Marxism

Biblically, all are privileged in some way over others. This includes the reality that many blacks, in one way or another, are privileged over other blacks. Those that are underprivileged in one way are often privileged in other ways; consequently, most people, including blacks, are both privileged and underprivileged depending on what is being compared. Privilege is not a sin in Scripture, but it can lead to sin (Luke 12:16–22; Jas 2:1–6). Privilege does not equal oppression or make a person an oppressor. Abraham was wealthy (Gen 24:35), Israel was privileged by being God's chosen nation (Rom 3:1–2), and Paul was privileged as a Roman citizen (Acts 16:37–38; 22:28).[16] God gave these privileges. The truth is that virtually everyone ex-

---

14. See Williams, *Race & Economics*, and Sowell, *Wealth, Poverty, and Politics*.

15. Mac Donald, *Diversity Delusion*, 207.

16. For example, Roman citizens could not be crucified.

periences privilege in comparison to someone else, and most experience a lack of privilege that others enjoy. These privileges can include things such as living in America, having a good family, having both father and mother in the home, wealth, health, geographical location, proximity to certain opportunities, and physical or mental abilities. For an example of black people from around the world seeking to come to America and become American citizens because of it being the best place for black people, listen to Ayaan Hirsi Ali.[17]

All true blessings, privileges, are ultimately from God and only require thanksgiving and good stewardship (Matt 25:14–30). But they are not sin, and, therefore, do not involve guilt or require repentance. In the parable of the talents, one man received one talent, another man received two, and the last one received five talents. Christ did not promote nor accuse the ones of supremacy or sinful privilege based on having more talents, thereby opportunity and privilege. Instead, as a matter of stewardship, they were judged on how they used their blessings, privileges. The same is true of how God judges each human, whether we are talking about spiritual blessings, privileges (Eph 1:3; 1 Cor 12:1), or common grace blessings (Matt 5:45). Biblically, blessings and privileges do not suggest repentance or guilt but stewardship before God and thankfulness (Luke 17:11–17).

Privilege and receiving blessings are not sins, nor do they make a person an oppressor, nor does the lack of them make one oppressed. But ungratefulness is a sin (Luke 6:35; Rom 1:21; 2 Tim 3:2). Using blessings and privileges to treat others as less than one created in the image of God is sin (Matt 7:12), as is treating one as not salvationally loved by God (John 3:16). Privilege and blessings require humility, thankfulness, and stewardship toward God and not repentance and guilt. Again, we see cultural Marxism and Christianity in absolute conflict. Therefore, relying on such an antithetical flawed theory and considering it a valuable analytical tool, as the promoters of Resolution 9 did (see chapter 9), is an egregious and dangerous error.

17. Robinson, "Case against Revolution."

26

4

Cultural Marxism's Explanation and Answer for Racism

The Oppressed According to Cultural Marxism

THE OPPRESSED ARE MINORITIES, which can include such groups as non-white people (predominantly blacks), non-Christians, homosexuals, and transgenders. A person is deemed to be oppressed if he belongs to a minority group even though the individual may never have personally experienced oppression or discrimination. For example, if a person is black and blacks are a minority, he is considered to suffer oppression because he is black regardless if he has been oppressed or not.

The Oppressors According to Cultural Marxism

The oppressors are majorities, which can include such groups as white people (especially white males), Christians, heterosexuals, and cisgenders (cisgender is a person whose gender identity corresponds to their sex at birth).[1] A person is considered an oppressor if he belongs to a majority group even if the individual has never acted oppressively or discriminatorily toward others. Also, if a person was a racist and later repented and confessed his past oppression as sin, he is still considered an oppressor because he is a part of an oppressive group. For example, a white person is a

1. A person born as a girl still sees herself as a girl, and likewise with a boy.

white supremacist because he is white, even if he never had a racist thought in his life. Even if he is in every conscious thought and act not a racist, he is, according to cultural Marxism and social justice, an implicit racist; that is to say, he is a racist unconsciously. Not even the gospel of Christ can deliver a white person from being a racist.

Biblical Evaluation of Cultural Marxism

Biblically, neither biology nor majority status determines whether a person is an oppressor. The color of a person's skin does not make a person a white supremacist. People who mistreat other people, demean other groups, view themselves as superior to others, or can rightly be called a white supremacist (or otherwise supremacist) do so because of their individual sin. Treating other human beings who are created in the image of God oppressively is the sin of pride (Lev 19:15; Matt 5:43–44; 22:39; Jas 2:1–6). It should be and can be repented of, and forgiveness sought for this and all other sins we are guilty of by trusting Christ as Savior (Rom 10:9–10). As a Christian, a person cannot be considered a supremacist of any kind unless he personally commits that sin after forgiveness in Christ. Then he can be forgiven by confessing that sin as he can be forgiven all sins committed after experiencing salvation (1 John 1:9).

According to Critical Race Theory, Who Can Be a Racist?

Only a person who belongs to the majority race or sex can be racist or sexist and exercise their power to oppress others. The required majority status is due to critical race theory sculpting racism to include an exercise of power by one group over another group, which is understood to preclude minorities from being capable of racism. Therefore, a black person cannot be a racist, and a woman cannot be a sexist as long as they are minorities.[2]

As a part of the majority, whites are racists and wrongfully privileged because they are white (especially white males). They are white supremacists and will always be white supremacists. Their whiteness and privilege as a white person make them sinners. They cannot, as long as they are white and the majority, be oppressed. There must be a redistribution

2. Women are not actually a minority in America, but they are often spoken of as though they are. https://www.census.gov/prod/cen2010/briefs/c2010br-03.pdf, accessed 7/17/20.

of wealth and power so that every group experiences the same results, even if individuals in the group do nothing to deserve the redistribution. For example, everyone should make the same amount and have the same privileges, even if some who can work do not. Cultural Marxism, of which critical race theory is a part, is about equal outcomes rather than equal opportunity for everyone. According to social justice, unequal outcomes equal injustice. The question of whether other factors that are not oppressive or due to white privilege (such as personal responsibility, desire, family makeup, socially inherited attitudes, geography, or different work ethics) contributed to some having more and some having less are either minimized or rejected outright.

Additionally, what is called white privilege is often better-labeled majority privilege. Some resist this because it undermines the claim of systemic racism. Many of the privileges of being white in America are really just the privileges associated with being the majority. As examples of white privilege, the promoters of systemic racism say whites can see people like themselves on television and in artwork, live in a neighborhood that they freely choose and among people like themselves, and work in jobs where they are not the only white person. They can be more comfortable and secure in more places in society and are more comfortable with many of the standards of society. But such things are true of the majority anywhere. If a white American moves to South Korea, he will experience what a black person often experiences living in a predominately white culture, but that does not make the Koreans racists. If a white and black person moved to Africa, the roles would be reversed of what they are in America, but that does not mean that Africa is systemically racist against white people, or that all Africans are racists because of the color of their skin or their majority status. ➤ Well, Africa didn't enslave black ppl like we did

Much of what is promoted as white privilege, which reinforces racial tensions and the idea that America is systemically racist (it is in America's DNA, and, therefore, irremovable without destroying the present system) is better understood as majority privilege. That is if we desire to promote racial harmony, which is not the desire of many. To recognize the difference between majority status and systemic racism is not to dismiss the presence of actual racism. I believe racism exists in America and that it is wrong, but I reject the claim of systemic racism.

Rather, it is to properly distinguish between genuine racism and what are merely the results of living in a culture where one's group is not the majority. Every person who moves to America experiences many of the same things as blacks (even more, i.e., having left their home and wealth and not knowing the language or culture), but it is not because of racism. It is the consequence of living in a society where one's group is a minority. A white or black person would have similar experiences if he moved to Taiwan. Further, the success of those who have immigrated to America reminds us that being a minority, poor, lacking political power, or not knowing the language or culture can be overcome because the obstacles to success are not necessarily due to racism, but merely the product of living in a culture as a minority. This reality reemphasizes that the benefits of the majority are not off-limits to minorities if they truly desire them and are willing to do the work to achieve them. Simply wanting them is not enough.

Additionally, some privileges are due to economic privilege (vast variations exist within each racial group), which can be experienced by those who both desire and work hard for them. That is to say, with greater financial success comes greater freedom to enjoy certain privileges in America; that is the nature of capitalism. We see examples of the accessibility of America's upward mobility among minorities in immigrant populations like the Jews, Cubans, Asians, and Indians. We also witness the attainment of such privilege within the black community by those who have accepted the requirement of personal responsibility and America's capitalistic requirements for financial advancement. These values are not white. Rather, they are American capitalism's values, much of which emanates from biblical teaching such as the ten commandments (Exod 20: 1–17; see also 1 Thess 4:11; 2 Thess 3:10). I reiterate this not to say there is no prejudice or racism in America. It is to say that I do not believe it is systemic. Therefore, although the presence of racism presents a significant obstacle for some that we should desire to eliminate, it is not sufficient to stop a person, regardless of race, from advancing in America. The success of millions of minorities, including blacks, in America, stands as a perennial refutation of the claim that America is systemically racist (it is in America's DNA).

Some non-racial barriers to overcome are included in accepting the American values of obeying the law, meritocracy, competency, and proper preparation for a job. While those in the majority should be sensitive to the disparities and difficulties a minority may experience that the majority does not, the majority does not have to feel guilty or accept the title racist or believe that America is systemically racist. Christians should be at the forefront of empathizing with the struggles of those in the minority, but this does not include white guilt, the absurd idea of reparations and repentance for what others have done, or becoming woke. *← charged terms periodically*

Walter E. Williams argues, "The most difficult problems black Americans face, particularly those who are poor, cannot adequately be explained by current racial discrimination. Instead, most problems are self-inflicted or . . . a result of policies, regulations, and restrictions emanating from federal, state, and local governments."[3] He is referring primarily to the government's involvement in the economy through socialistic measures. Thomas Sowell contends there is no place on earth where there are equal outcomes.[4]

Biblical Evaluation of Critical Race Theory

Biblically, anyone can be racist or commit any other sin that other humans can commit if they are physically and mentally able. Anyone who commits any sin can be forgiven and given a new life through trusting Jesus Christ and his sacrifice on the cross for their sin (John 3:1–4, 16; Rom 10:9–19; 1 Cor 15:1–4). Racism is not determined by one's group size or skin color, but by their heart beliefs that are reflected in their actions. Sin originates internally in the heart rather than externally in skin color, group associations, or even in a sinful act (Matt 12:34; 15:38). For example, murder or adultery (Mark 7:21; Matt 5:27–32) is a sinful desire of the heart even if there is no physical murder or adultery. But if the person commits the physical act, the heart sin is compounded by the overt sin (Jas 1:15).

Groups can sin against groups

Correcting Racism According to Cultural Marxism

Since racism is systemic, it will probably take total destruction of the present structures, which will probably mean uncivil methods like anarchical behavior, rioting and destroying private property, killing, revolt, or a complete violent revolution. The systemic racism is so thorough that it may be impossible to remove the racist nature of American culture through a Republican-Democratic structure of government and ordinary, civil, democratic politics. This bourgeoning mindset is demonstrated in the Democratic Party by some who carry out anti-civil or even violent behavior and others who minimize that type of action. Speaking of the ultimate

---

3. Williams, *Race & Economics*, 7.
4. Sowell, "Myths of Economic Inequality."

outcome of critical race theory, Dr. E. S. Williams states, "The only meaningful consequence that this wide application [of cultural Marxism] could possibly ever have is the marginalization of traditional European culture."[5] Of course, this includes anything noble associated with Christianity or its influence on culture. When we stand against social justice, we do so not just to protect America or capitalism as important as they are; we are fighting for the purity of the gospel and religious liberty to live out our faith.

According to cultural Marxism, the majority is the oppressor of the minority, which is the oppressed. The goal is not merely an equal opportunity or equality before the law, but rather it is an equal outcome for all. Therefore, there must be a total overturning of society to obtain equality of outcome. For example, Dr. E. S. Williams says, "If cisgender people (a person whose gender identity corresponds to the sex they were identified at birth—i.e., biologically) are oppressors, the solution is to encourage transgenderism."[6] This perspective would include gender fluidity and all that entails. If heterosexuality is oppressive, then promote homosexuality. If whites are oppressive, promote minorities and white guilt for being privileged. The correction of white oppression requires the redistribution of wealth and power, even if it is forced redistribution.

There is no personal redemption in this life if you are a white person in the sense of total redemption, forgiveness, and deliverance so that you cease to be inherently racist, because there will always be racism, and you are a white person.[7] That is why they use the term "white supremacist" to refer, not to some extreme sector of the white population as has been done historically, but white people as a whole.[8] Becoming woke (seeing things through the eyes of the oppressed, which often means virtually every disadvantage or lack of success is attributable to racism) may help. Still, even that does not afford complete redemption and removal of the stain of guilt and racism for a white person.

---

5. Thenewcalvinist, "Stain," 11:26–35.

6. Thenewcalvinist, "Stain," 10:08–12.

7. Unless, possibly, the white population became the minority group.

8. The term "white supremacy," meaning that whites historically viewed themselves and have been viewed as inherently superior to blacks (true racism), has been used by people in the past. I believe the term is still an overstatement since this would not have been true of all white people in the past and is most assuredly not true today. Additionally, in modern times and until recently, the pervasive usage in American culture referred to what is now known as alt-right groups such as skinheads, Nazis, and other white supremacists. Steele, *White Guilt*, 99.

Hawk Newsome, chairman of the greater New York Black Lives Matter (BLM, I use this abbreviation for the group, slogan, and chant) movement, speaking about the movement's goals and actions, gives a clear example of cultural Marxism. He said in an interview with Martha MacCallum, "If this country doesn't give us what we want, then we will burn down this system and replace it. All right? And I could be speaking figuratively; I could be speaking literally. It's a matter of interpretation."[9] I believe he left it open to interpretation to avoid being charged with inciting to riot. His final statement in the interview seems to make clear what he meant. He said, "I just want black liberation and sovereignty *by any means necessary*"[10] (italics added).

Regarding violence, James Cone, the father of Black Liberation Theology, which is heretical theology, says, "The Christian does not decide between violence and non-violence, evil and good. He decides between the lesser and the greater evil. He must ponder whether revolutionary violence is less or more deplorable than the violence perpetuated by the system."[11] Similar to Newsome, Cone speaks of black liberation as the "emancipation of black people from white oppression *by whatever means black people deem necessary*"[12] (italics added).

Isn't this what American revolutionaries did?.

The Biblical Evaluation of Cultural Marxism

Biblically, the cause of genuine racism is sin, pride, and showing partiality where none should exist. Actual racism, in contrast to cultural Marxism or popular racism, exists when a person views his race or ethnicity as inherently superior to another race. As with all sin, the forgiveness of actual racism requires repentance and faith in Christ that results in total forgiveness (John 3:16) and regeneration (1 Pet 1:23).[13] Then the redeemed must walk in the Word and the power of the Holy Spirit of God (Gal 5:16). The answer to the sin of racism is the same as the answer for all other sins, even blasphemy (Matt 12:30–32) or murdering the pre-born (1 John 1:9).

---

9. Freedom Forum, "MacCallum Interviews Newsome," 2:40–54.

10. Freedom Forum, "MacCallum Interviews Newsome," 6:05–09.

11. Cone, *Black Theology*, 143.

12. Cone, *Black Theology and Black Power*, 121.

13. Repentance is turning from sin and faith is turning to Christ. They are two aspects of one change of mind, act, that results in salvation, which is all by grace.

5

An Insight into How Cultural Marxism and Social Justice Work

IT IS ESSENTIAL TO keep the following thoughts in mind as we consider how cultural Marxism and social justice work in real-life situations or crises like the death of George Floyd and the ensuing anarchy.[1] First, some injustices that social justice warriors deem an injustice and cultural Marxists stand against are actual injustices. Many who are not social justice warriors may see the same event and also conclude it is an injustice that needs to be corrected.[2] Consequently, even those who hold opposing beliefs may unite against real injustice. Furthermore, just because others fight the same injustice does not mean that cultural Marxists are not involved, employing their strategies or seeking their ultimate goal of overthrowing capitalism

1. The backdrop of this chapter was the death of George Floyd and resulting riots and anarchy that spread across America in 2020, but the explanations of how social justice works are applicable to similar events of racial conflict and rioting.

2. The Conservative Baptist Network provided a thoroughly Christian response to the George Floyd event. The statement equally condemned both the injustice by the police against George Floyd and the injustices resulting from some people who seek justice for the death of George Floyd by inflicting injustices on innocent people's lives and livelihood. Conservative Baptist Network. "Statement Regarding George Floyd."

In contrast, the Southern Baptist Convention statement condemned the injustice by the police against George Floyd, but it failed to include condemnation of the injustices resulting from some people who seek justice for the death of George Floyd by inflicting injustices on innocent people's lives and livelihood. Christians should stand against *all* injustices. To be against one actual injustice and ignore other actual injustices is to fail to respond in a thoroughly Christian manner. Baptist Press Staff, "Southern Baptist Leaders Issue Joint Statement."

and America. We should always keep foremost in our minds that the overthrow of America includes the banning of Christianity and the spreading of the gospel.[3]

The motive and the methods utilized by social justice advocates (many of whom are Marxists) in attempting to right a wrong can be very different from those of ordinary citizens. Some social justice advocates may use anarchist tactics that are approved of and promoted by social justice advocates who are not actually on the streets. These advocates are in academia, newsrooms, and places of power.[4]

In an interview, Dr. Richard Pipes, the "acclaimed historian and Harvard University professor of Sovietology . . . who [also] served on the National Security Council during the Reagan administration,"[5] explained that there are not as many communists among academics as some think. Still, these academics are significantly sympathetic to Marxist ideas. He explained the situation as follows.

> While academic leftists, and I'd include their media allies, are not communists, they are anti-anti-communists. In other words, they have contempt for right-wingers, conservative, or libertarians who are anti-communists. Why? Academic leftists and their media allies agree with many of the stated goals of communism, such as the equal distribution of wealth, income equality, and other goals spelled out in Karl Marx and Friedrich Engels' "Manifesto of the Communist Party."[6]

Consequently, when we ask how many Marxists are in academia, we will get the wrong answer because we have asked the wrong question. When I was in graduate school at Henderson State University, I asked the head of the sociology department how many sociologists were capitalists, socialists, and communists. He responded, "Ninety percent are socialists, and ten percent are communists." I immediately asked what about those that are capitalists? He said, "They are not statistically significant."[7]

Social justice advocates seek the destruction of America's capitalistic civil system as a necessary component to usher in a socialistic Utopia.

---

3. Of course, this would include all supernatural faiths since Marxism is a materialistic faith.

4. Chamberlain, "Riots Break Out."

5. Williams, *Liberty Versus the Tyranny*, 24.

6. Williams, *Liberty Versus the Tyranny*, 24.

7. I attended Henderson State University in Arkansas from 1986–88.

Harvard professor Cornel West's remarks after the death of George Floyd and the riots that followed condemns America's capitalistic system as a failure.

West says, "I think we are witnessing America as a *failed social experiment.* And what I mean by that is that the history of black people for over 200-something years in America has been looking at America's failure. Its capitalist economy could not generate and deliver in such a way that people could live lives of decency. The nation-state, its criminal justice system, its legal system could not generate protection of rights and liberties"[8] (italics added).

Notice that the rioters and looters are not to blame because everything happening is due to racial injustice, which is the Marxian paradigm. The social justice intellectuals make the academic arguments for abandoning capitalism for socialism, while the social justice warriors on the street provide the terrorizing fear needed, and the white guilted Americans supply the unjustified sympathy and leniency for those who destroy private property and kill innocent people. Those who are not social justice advocates but who also see the injustice usually seek justice through the legal, legislative, and elective processes.

Shelby Steele explains white guilt as "the *vacuum of moral authority* that comes from simply *knowing* that one's race is associated with racism. Whites (and American institutions) must acknowledge historical racism to show themselves redeemed of it, but once they acknowledge it, they lose moral authority over everything having to do with race, equality, social justice, poverty, and so on . . . The authority they lose transfers to the 'victims' of historical racism and becomes their great power in society. This is why white guilt is quite literally the same thing as black power."[9]

Steele does not use white guilt to mean moral guilt. Instead, it is a willingness by white people and their institutions to do almost anything to avoid the stigmatization of being called racist. Steele maintains that white guilt produces only results like affirmative action.[10] For example, rather

8. Chamberlain, "Riots Break Out," paras. 5–6.

9. Steele, *White Guilt,* 24.

10. Outcomes look at the problem, like not having many black students in college, and answer the problem by such outcome approaches as affirmative action or diversity emphasis. However, outside of the presence of actual racism, outcome answers do not address the real problem, which may be such things as a lack of excellent primary and secondary schools to attend, out-of-wedlock pregnancies, cultural values that favor rappers or criminals more than those who prioritize getting a good education, and hard work.

than a university accepting the 2 or 3 percent of black students who are qualified on their own merit (SAT scores), the university may set a standard (quota) of admitting 7 percent of black students. This approach results in a predominately white institution doing whatever is needed, such as lowering standards, to make sure it reaches its quota. By reaching its quota, the university effectively protects itself from the stigma of being racist, even if some are accepted who cannot do the work that will be required in class. The university can say, see how many black students we have; therefore, we are not racists.

An example of the damage such quotas cause can be seen when, because of affirmative action, a black student is accepted into a university like Harvard or Cornell in which the student would not do well but would do well in 90 percent of the universities in America. To say some are accepted who are not able to do the work required in certain universities is not racist because I can say the same about me and countless other white students. Affirmative action detrimentally mismatches student capabilities with particular university requirements in order to meet the school's quota, which serves the purpose of insulating the university from the stigma of being a racist institution, even at the expense of the black students. Not only does it hurt the students who would have been academically better suited at a different university, but it also hurts the black students who were accepted on their own merit. Such practices are self-serving for white people (showing they are not racists) and denigrating to black people; it also maintains the patronizing white deliverer model.

Regrettably, I see white guilt in some of the SBC leadership as well when they emphasize color-based selection rather than merit-based.[11] Such is no less dishonoring to our black brothers and sisters than when secular society does it. It is racist not to select a black person who is the most qualified in both skillset and doctrine simply because he is black, and it is racism motivated by white guilt to choose lesser qualified blacks because of the color of their skin. As equal image-bearers of God, I assure you, we have many qualified black people to speak and serve without resorting to guilt-motivated paternalism.

For example, some of the best preachers on planet earth are doctrinally sound black preachers—such as Dr. Lee Brand and Voddie Baucham. We do not have to compromise doctrinally to find black preachers to endorse.

---

11. I have heard and read some calls for more diversity with no mention of qualified diversity.

We need not compromise by hiring black scholars who are supportive of such ideas as critical race theory and intersectionality in order to demonstrate we are not racists; to do so dishonors black scholars who have not so compromised, but, most of all, it dishonors Christ. There is nothing wrong, and everything right, with doing due diligence to make sure we are not using lesser qualified white leaders because of convenience while overlooking qualified conservative black preachers and scholars. But it is pandering and racist to choose or reject people based on skin color regardless of how sincere the motive.

Speaking of white guilt, Steele says, "It constantly portrays problems of minority under development as problems of injustice."[12] That is precisely what cultural Marxism does. White guilt results in creating such things as the Great Society and affirmative action, and now permitting the grossest of anarchical criminal behavior while decreasing funding of police at one of the most violent times in American history all in an attempt to abolish America.[13] All the while blaming everyone but the perpetrators of the anarchist action, which is often referred to by the left as protests or mostly peaceful protests. As a result, blacks are dehumanized, and the government has abandoned its primary responsibility of protecting its citizenry.

Significant black scholars and intellectuals such as Larry Elder, Thomas Sowell, Shelby Steele, Robert L. Woodson Sr., Walter Williams, Jason Riley, and Glenn Loury, as well as many other black people, are calling for personal responsibility as the principal answer to the problems in the black community.[14] As we have seen, that is contrary to the message of social justice and cultural Marxism, which bases everything on group identity instead of individual responsibility.

Social justice blames any lack of success in the black community on systemic racial injustice. Social justice warriors and the woke do not ask if racism is present; they always assume its presence. The author of *White Fragility*, Robin DiAngelo, states it this way: "The question is not '*did* racism

---

12. Steele, *White Guilt*, 64.

13. "The Great Society was an ambitious series of policy initiatives, legislation, and programs spearheaded by President Lyndon B. Johnson with the main goals of ending poverty, reducing crime, abolishing inequality and improving the environment." "Great Society," para. 1.

14. Many black people of all ages and backgrounds are saying the same. See https://www.facebook.com/nancy.rogerscrosby/videos/10220521552061505/UzpfSTEwM-DAzMDY1NDc1MTIoNTozMDA3MDY2NDc2Mjc4MjU/ and https://www.facebook.com/nancy.rogerscrosby/videos/10220497769746962/?fref=mentions.

take place'? but rather '*how did* racism manifest in that situation?'"[15] In such an environment, even to ask for evidence of systemic racism results in being called a racist, and white guilt keeps many white people from asking since they will do anything to avoid being labeled a racist.

Moreover, systemic racism cannot be demonstrated to be in existence today by referring to the past, such as the times of slavery, Jim Crow (laws enacted to enforce segregation), or other events predating legal corrections.[16] Nor can it be evidenced by merely providing examples of actual racism, as people are prone to do. Systemic racism could be demonstrated by exposing the existence of legal discrimination, as has been true in the past. This demonstration would require laws that explicitly prohibit black people from something white people are permitted based solely on race. For example, prior to the civil rights movement of the 1960s, blacks were not allowed to eat in many white restaurants because it was illegal.

Consequently, if you have the courage, ask those who argue for the existence of systemic racism to define what they mean and to provide *incontrovertible empirical data* to prove systemic racism exists; that would include the idea that there are no other plausible reasons or factors to be considered. For example, cab drivers and pizza delivery drives have been accused of racism for picking up a white customer and passing by a black customer. Or for refusing to make home pizza deliveries in a black area. But these facts alone do not prove racism, although the woke use such to show rampant racism. The truth is that many times, in these situations, the drivers or the taxicab commissioner who restricts the drivers are black themselves. Many of the drivers who refuse to make home pizza deliveries live in the very neighborhoods where they refuse to make deliveries. They do so not because of racism but because they fear for their safety. It is hard to make the case that black drivers and commissioners are racist against black people.[17]

This should remind us to consider other factors before we join the racism frenzy of the woke and race-baiters. Additionally, for them to seek to substantiate the presence of systemic racism by saying such things as we know it does, or if you were black, you would know. Or to provide verifiable anecdotal evidence only proves some racism exists (which no one denies),

15. DiAngelo, "Anti-Racism Handout."

16. Many legal corrections have been passed such as the Civil Rights Act of 1964, Voting Rights Act of 1965, and the Fair Housing Act of 1968.

17. Williams, *Race & Economics*, 119–21.

but it does not demonstrate systemic racism. In a fallen world, there will always be various forms of ungodly discrimination, not just racial. An important follow-up question that should be asked is if racism is systemic, what will it take to eliminate it, and how will we know it has been eliminated? Be specific.

Thomas Sowell demonstrates how, after slavery ended, blacks increased their income at a faster rate than whites even though they had to confront many agreements made by whites to keep them down. By 1900, their incomes were one-half again higher than they were in 1867. They increased their earnings faster than the nation as a whole.[18] The significance of this is that despite the egregious wrongs inflicted on them by whites, blacks still excelled. This is not to justify the ill-treatment of blacks by whites, but rather to highlight that blacks can excel even under dire circumstances because they, like whites, are created in the image of God.

Since the victories of the civil rights movement of the sixties, black militants, many of whom are Marxists, have used white guilt to advance their cause of making white people and their institutions responsible for the black people's well-being and success, instead of promoting personal responsibility for how they fare in their newfound freedom. Liberal politicians, a host of business, community, and religious leaders have been willing to do anything out of white guilt to avoid the dreaded stigmatism of being called a racist. Using white guilt to advance black people is not to be understood as the approach that all black people have adopted, but many militants, along with leaders like Reverend Sharpton and Jesse Jackson, have.

This method is as Marxian and demeaning to blacks today as it was in the riots of the sixties.[19] These social justice warriors will speak about injustices being the cause of problems in the black community a myriad of times for each time they make even the slightest public reference to calling on black people to take personal responsibility. This is not a gross generalization of all blacks because many in the black community take responsibility for their lives and work hard at developing their family and their jobs. The Blexit movement (Black exit from the Democratic Party) was begun by Candace (:s and Brandon Tatum to set black people free from the oppression of the Democratic party and the social justice warriors.[20]

---

18. Hoover Institution, "Discrimination and Disparities," 13:30–47.

19. Steele, *White Guilt*, 30–33.

20. See https://blexitfoundation.org/.

Walter E. Williams comments, "The experience of several ethnic minority groups in the United States and elsewhere seriously calls into question arguments that disadvantaged minorities in the United States *must* acquire political power and need measures to 'end racism' in order for socioeconomic growth to occur."[21] He further states, "There is little evidence that race-based discrimination is widespread in today's America."[22] This is in stark contrast to the continued paradigm presented by liberals, BLM, and the woke that America is systemically racist. In other words, it is in our DNA. Unfortunately, this includes some leaders in the SBC.

Steele says, "Wherever and whenever there is white guilt, a terrible illusion prevails: that social justice is not a condition but an agent. In this illusion, social justice procures an entirely better life for people apart from their own efforts. Therefore, it makes sense for minorities to make social justice a priority over their individual pursuit of education and wealth . . . The reason for this illusion is that white guilt *wants no obligation to minority developments*. It needs only the *display* of social justice to win moral authority. It gets no credit when blacks independently develop themselves."[23] The truth is that neither the end of slavery nor the gains of the civil rights movement led by Martin Luther King guarantee success for black people. They only provide the opportunity for it, but the necessary agent is the person taking responsibility for his life and future; this requirement is the same for both whites and blacks.

One need not look far for the presence of white guilt during the time of anarchy following the death of Floyd. For example, in reference to the riots following the death of George Floyd, Democrat Governor Gavin Newsom said, "The black community is not responsible for what is happening right now. We are—our institutions are—accountable to this moment."[24] The Democrat Attorney General of Massachusetts is Maura Healy. She described the rioting by saying, "Yes, America is burning, but that's how forests grow."[25] Two days after looters destroyed stores, Democrat Teresa Mosquera of the Seattle City Council, said, "Colleagues, I hope we're all

21. Williams, *Race & Economics*, 15.

22. Williams, *Race & Economics*, 133. He demonstrates how crime, breakdown of the family, morals, poor education, and a host of economic non-racial considerations play a significant role in what is mischaracterized as racist issues.

23. Steele, *White Guilt*, 63.

24. Angst, "Your Rage Is Real," para. 2.

25. Schoenberg, "America Is Burning," para. 1.

saying we understand why that destruction happened and we understand why people are upset."[26] This is reminiscent of John Kerry's degrading white guilt comment many years ago. Walter Williams recalls, "In a campaign speech before a predominantly black audience, in reference to so many blacks in prison, presidential candidate John Kerry said, 'That's unacceptable, but it's not their fault.'"[27] White guilt is racist since operating out of white guilt is to first and foremost benefit white people by doing whatever it takes to avoid being called a racist; it gives the appearance of caring and sympathy, but it is actually more about protecting oneself at the expense of others. It degrades black people by holding them to a lower standard of personal responsibility than the situation warrants and is inappropriate for one created in the image of God. It is racist. Further, social justice is as racist as white guilt because it judges a person by their skin color to either be guilty or innocent.

An example of associating such disparate groups as social justice advocates and non-social justice advocates can be seen in the almost universal agreement on the apparent[28] injustice of the death of George Floyd.[29] But the means for seeking justice by cultural Marxists and those who view the death of Floyd as a heinous act but love America are categorically different.[30] The latter group sees Floyd's death as well as the wanton destruction of innocent lives and their property through rioting and looting as injustices. Social justice advocates view wanton destruction of innocents and their livelihood as a means to their goal. The social justice perspective vividly reminds us that what some call social justice is better described as socialistic justice.

To only oppose *either* the injustice against Floyd or the injustice perpetrated by the rioters against innocents is the very kind of partial and biased justice the rioters claim to be protesting. They are employing the very sort of partial justice to make their case that they say they are against. Christians must stand unequivocally against the injustice against Floyd and

---

26. Murdock, "Looting and Rioting," para. 6.

27. Williams, *Liberty Versus the Tyranny*, 341.

28. I use the word "apparent" only because at the time of this writing, while every indication is that the officer did unjustifiably cause the death of George Floyd (something I agree with based on what we know at this time), there may still be unknown facts, which could alter or ameliorate the case. I am not ready to abandon the legal system of due process, as flawed as it may be, for a tragic system of trial by the internet.

29. Murdock, "Rioters Do Injustice."

30. Chandler, "Pastors Urge Prayer" and Murdock, "Rioters Do Injustice."

the injustice committed by the rioters against the innocents. We stand unashamedly for God's impartial justice.

Second, to use the terms cultural Marxism and social justice to describe an event, group, or person does not necessarily mean that everyone involved is a card-carrying cultural Marxist or social justice warrior or even would describe themselves as such. Social justice warriors will welcome non-social justice warriors to join their fight, and they will join non-social justice warriors in their cause so long as it fits the overall plan of social justice advocates.

Using these terms to speak about an event does not necessarily signify that some acts of violence, anarchy, or civil disobedience are driven *exclusively* by cultural Marxism. Nor do they preclude non-cultural Marxists from getting caught up in the emotion of the moment and rioting alongside the social justice warriors. But even the acts that are not solely driven by cultural Marxists are promoted and used by them to further their cause, which is the destruction of American society and culture in order to usher in their dream of a socialistic Utopia. Such behavior by anyone facilitates their plan. We ignore these somewhat complex traits of how cultural Marxism and social justice work to our natural and spiritual peril.

BLM is the powerhouse behind many of the protests and riots.[31] BLM is a Marxist-run organization. Patrisse Cullors claims that she and Alicia Garza are "trained Marxists."[32] The call to defund police departments across the nation was initiated and promoted by BLM. It is a Marxist plan to further deconstruct American society to usher in a Marxist society. The BLM website says, "We call for a national defunding of police."[33] But may we ask, who will protect innocent people from criminals and rioters such as the BLM constituency? The criminals and rioters?[34]

The most prominent claim of systemic racism relates to the charge that the police are disproportionately killing blacks or even hunting down

---

31 Antifa is also involved with BLM in the rioting. Antifa is a loosely organized effort to fight what they see as fascism. They are, in fact, a very leftwing group of pro-socialists and communists who use the term fascism so broadly that it can encompass a vast array of ideas they oppose. They will often wrongly categorize love for America, patriotic acts, and words as fascism. They ignore the fact that America fought a costly world war against fascism and defeated it.

32. The Real News Network, "Short History of Black Lives Matter," 7:10. See also John, "Black Lives Matter Co-Founder Confirms."

33. Black Lives Matter, "#DefundThePolice," para. 8.

34. See Appendix 1 for eight reasons against defunding police departments.

blacks just to kill them. Therefore, the police are so corrupt and systemically racist, they must be destroyed. But while the media optics give credence to that claim, the facts do not.

Relying on data from the FBI, the Kaiser Foundation, and Statistical Research Inc, Edward Ring says,

> In 2018 a total of 209 blacks were killed by police, the overwhelming majority of them armed. This compares to 399 whites killed by police in that year . . . The root of the claim of a police war on blacks comes down to this: If you're black, in 2018 you had a one in 190,000 chance of having a fatal encounter with police, and if you're white, your chances of the same were only one in 495,000. Hence you will hear that blacks are 2.5 times as likely to be killed by police as whites.
>
> If that were all there was to it, perhaps there'd be a reason for more concern. But here are facts that cannot be ignored: blacks commit more crimes. In terms of arrests, blacks are twelve times as likely as whites to be arrested for murder, three times as likely for rape, eleven times as likely for robbery, and four times as likely for aggravated assault.
>
> This brings us back to the crux of the issue, which is whether police encounters with blacks result in a disproportionate number of fatalities. If you look at the death per arrest rate, they do not. In 2018 (these statistics are fairly consistent from year to year) the chances of dying while being arrested were exactly the same for whites and blacks, a nearly infinitesimal 1/100th of 1 percent.[35]

An Obama administration study in which the research team was comprised of mostly doctors so that the injuries could be medically assessed found the following. Out of 1,041,737 calls to the police for service, only 893 resulted in any level of use of force (UOF) by the police. That is a rate of 0.086 percent (eighty-six one-thousandths). Most of the force used was physical or conducted electrical weapons (CEWs, such as tasers). Firearms were used only six times. Out of these police and citizen encounters, only sixteen resulted in moderate to severe injury to a suspect, and there was only one fatality. Based on the facts of their research, they concluded, "Police UOF is rare. When force is used, officers most commonly rely on unarmed physical force and CEWs. Significant injuries are rare."[36]

35. Ring, "Black Athlete Stand Up?," paras. 9–11. The article provides a chart using data from the FBI, Kaiser Foundation, and Statista Research Inc.

36. The abstract shows the percentage of various uses of force and injuries sustained. Many hospitalizations were not due to injuries associated with the arrest but rather were

Whether racism is a factor in the death rate of criminals on the part of the police requires considering many factors other than a raw statistic or skin color. For example, it matters what the nature of the encounters between police with whites and blacks were. Did they all include an equal amount of violent crimes? What is the crime rate of the area in which the arrests were made? Did the clothing or behavior of the individual mimic others who attacked or killed a police officer in a previous arrest? Did the individual resist arrest or comply? Did the suspect have a criminal record or even a violent criminal record? Had the suspect acted violently against police before? Did the suspect have a weapon or appear to reach for one? Such factors do not prove the officer made a righteous arrest and use of deadly force, although they may. But they can demonstrate the use of force did not stem from racism.

The fact that a white officer killed a black criminal is insufficient to show racism, and that is a fact. Jumping to conclusions is not right for anyone, but particularly for a Christian. Let all the facts be examined before a judgment is made. We know all too well that when time is given for all the facts to surface, the once apparent racial incident can actually be devoid of racism. If the facts demonstrate discrimination, Christians should be the first to oppose it. If they do not, Christians should say so. In either case, Christians should resist the BLM zeitgeist that a white on black arrest or use of force, and by that fact alone, proves racism.

When people are confused about why the black rioters kill innocent blacks and destroy the private property of black citizens, they fail to understand the goal of Marxism is to demonstrate America is a failed system and needs to be replaced with socialism. Walter Williams notes the way people compare capitalism and Marxism is that "Often when people evaluate capitalism, they evaluate a system that exists on Earth. When they evaluate communism, they are talking about a non-existent Utopia. What exists on Earth with all of its problems and shortcomings, is always going to fail miserably when compared to a Utopia."[37]

Even if BLM was not so brazenly forthright about who they are and their agenda, anyone should be able to see that defunding police departments is insanity unless you are trying to destroy society as it is. That is precisely what the cultural Marxists are seeking to accomplish. The idea

---

self-inflicted by the one arrested. Bozeman et al., "Injuries Associated with Police." See also Ordway, "Police Use of Force."

37. Williams, *Liberty Versus the Tyranny*, 25.

that racism is systemic (used to mean comprehensively infected) means social structures must be destroyed and replaced. Thus, they employ anarchy to accomplish the destruction of America and capitalism, which (theoretically) will lead to the dream of a socialistic society of equal outcomes. The cultural Marxists first destroyed private and public property. Then they destroyed secular statues and monuments, which was soon followed by the destruction of churches and religious symbols, all as they declare Black Lives Matter.[38]

The destructive rewriting and degrading of American history, emphasizing only the failures, all while obscuring and banishing the heroism, sacrifice, and the good of American history, is an essential part of the Marxist plan. Marxism cannot take over a strong, knowledgeable, moral, spiritual, and patriotic country. Those churches who have forsaken "Thus says the Lord" for beliefs and rhetoric that are more suitable for a Tupperware party, or they even trumpet the message of woke socialistic justice, have contributed to American's vulnerability to Marxism.

Our public education system has failed at both the primary and secondary level, where objective Christian morality, American history, and patriotism have all but vanished, inadequately preparing our children for further education and life. Add to this that our liberal, socialistic, and Marxian centered academia has promoted socialism, decried faith, belittled patriotism, and demeaned capitalism for decades.[39] This academic climate has provided the needed pro-socialist intellectuals to frame the necessary arguments for socialism and against capitalism. The rioters in the street provide the required fear in the hearts of conservatives who then cave to white guilt and seek refuge in selfish suburbanism, wokeness, and tawdry clichés. Resultantly, America is a weakened opponent against Marxism. Given what I have seen and heard, I am not sure whether even all that we now know about BLM will convince the woke white evangelicals to disabuse themselves of identifying with BLM chants, marches, and clothing, although I pray it will.

I understand there is a difference between the declaration BLM and the organization of BLM. To wit, some who support the declaration do not support the organization. However, it seems to be unwise and unnecessary to opt for even the declaration BLM. First, as Christians, we must communicate our message clearly so that the listener knows who we are and what

---

38. All of this began to take place in 2020. See Rousselle, "Churches in 6 States."

39. See my book *Death of Man as Man*.

we represent and do not represent. It is virtually impossible to make clear who supports the declaration BLM and the organization and who just supports the declaration, at least, on anything other than a direct or personal level of conversation. If a person is echoing BLM, carrying a BLM sign, wearing BLM clothing, or painting BLM on something, it is almost impossible for observers to know whether he supports the declaration only or the declaration and the organization.

Second, as Christians, we have the privilege and stewardship of exalting God, Scripture, and the gospel by declaring an unambiguous message that all people are created by God and in his image, and, therefore, all lives are sacred—matter. BLM may say BLM, but it does not tell us why or how much, whereas the Christian message does both.

Third, the two most significant civil rights movements in American history were not based on a potentially confusing slogan that only elevates lives with a specific skin color without telling why they matter, to whom they matter, or how much they matter. These two civil rights advances were based on declaring the truth of Scripture and the Declaration of Independence. In his famous Gettysburg Address, Abraham Lincoln said, "Four score and seven years ago our fathers brought forth on this continent, a new nation, conceived in Liberty, and dedicated to the proposition that all men are created equal."[40] His timeline leads not to the Constitution but to the Declaration of Independence, which says, "We hold these truths to be self-evident, that all men are created equal, that they are endowed by their Creator with certain unalienable Rights."[41]

In like manner, the Civil Rights movement of the 1960s was based on a Christian worldview. Martin Luther King Jr. quoted the Declaration of Independence in his iconic "I Have a Dream" speech, saying "I have a dream that one day this nation will rise up and live out the true meaning of its creed: '*We hold these truths to be self-evident, that all men are created equal.*'"[42] Why would we, as Christians, do less?

Additionally, I am not advocating saying "all lives matter" in place of BLM. Because without the why of being created in the image of God, it is equally inadequate. We must declare all lives matter because all humans are created in the image of God. When we say that, we are saying there is one human race created by God in his image, of which all have sinned, and for

---

40. Lincoln, "Gettysburg Address," para. 1.
41. See the American Declaration of Independence.
42. King, "I Have a Dream," para. 17.

whom Christ died because God loves every person. That declaration leads to only one place, the gospel. Why would we unnecessarily encumber this message?

Thomas Sowell summarizes the seriousness of it all. Sowell was a guest on *Life Liberty & Levin*. Mark Levin asked his thoughts about what is going on in America. Sowell responded, "I must say, even though I'm regarded as pessimistic, I was never pessimistic enough to think that things would degenerate to the point where they are now. Where adult human beings are talking about getting rid of the police. Where they're talking about reducing the number of police, reducing the resources put into police work at a time when murder rates have been skyrocketing over what they were just a year ago, 2019."[43] He went on to say, "We may well reach a point of no return."[44] He illustrated this with the fall of Rome.

He later said, "If the election goes to Biden, there's a good chance that the Democrats will then control the two branches of Congress and the White House, and considering the kinds of things that they are proposing, that could well be the point of no return for this country."[45]

Steele became involved in the militant movement of the sixties, and he says that is where he first encountered Marxian concepts like "raise your consciousness" and "the Marxian idea of social determinism."[46] He speaks of the militants of the sixties who embraced these concepts saying, "This essentially Marxist vision of American racism . . . was the precursor to the now-common argument that racism is 'systemic,' 'structural' and 'institutional.'"[47]

He distinguishes the new militant approach in the sixties from Martin Luther King's approach, which believed "racism was simply a barrier, a tragic aberration, in an America that was otherwise essentially open and fair."[48] This new militant approach would not emphasize personal responsibility but "social determinism."[49] That remains the approach of BLM and other cultural Marxists of our day.

---

43. Levin, "Thomas Sowell on Utter Madness," 0:52–1:25.

44. Levin, "Thomas Sowell on Utter Madness," 1:51–53.

45. Levin, "Thomas Sowell Discusses 'Systemic Racism,'" 2:45–3:07.

46. Steele, *White Guilt*, 31 and 32 respectively.

47. Steele, *White Guilt*, 31 or 32.

48. Steele, *White Guilt*, 32.

49. Steele, *White Guilt*, 32.

Social determinism is the idea that such things as external social factors, structures, laws, politics, and systemic racism make people what they are. Think of it this way. Genetic determinism is the idea that you are a product of your genes. To wit, your behavior, successes, and morals, like your eye and hair color, are determined. Similarly, in social determinism, your behavior, morals, and achievements are determined solely by societal structures. Consequently, societal structures not only provide the opportunity for progress, but they are also the agency for progress. According to determinism, there is no free will (ability) to do otherwise at the moral moment of decision. Therefore, your plight is not the result of personal irresponsibility, nor can it be corrected by the individual taking personal responsibility. Instead, your situation changes because of the change in societal structures.

Note how rare it is to hear social justice warriors, their leaders, and liberal politicians calling black people to take personal responsibility for their choices and future. Social justice leaders' failure to call black people to take personal responsibility for their lives is utterly degrading because such failure treats them as less than beings created in the image of God. Although societal influences can make things more or less difficult, they are not determinative of what kind of person we become. This is no less true of black people than white people; we are all created in the image of God, and, therefore, essentially equal.

For the Christian, we can recognize the influence (even strongly so) of culture, law, and civil structures on people, but these influences do not determine what kind of person an individual will become. The determinative agent is the individual. We have that ability because we are created in the image of God. Think about how salvation changes a person regardless of the societal structure.

Steele says Martin Luther King is represented more by conservatives today than liberals or militants. He says,

> In fact, most of today's conservatives sound like Martin Luther King
> in 1963. Contemporary conservatism treats race with precisely the
> same compassionate Jefferson Liberalism that Martin Luther King
> articulated in his "I Have a Dream" speech. Is there, on the right, a
> covert, unspoken loyalty to racial hierarchy, a quiet atavistic com-
> mitment to white supremacy? In the hearts of some, there must be.
> There are fools and devils everywhere. But today's right has made

itself *accountable* to the democratic and *moral* vision of the early Martin Luther King.[50]

The peaceful personal responsibility approach versus the political, social justice warrior approach even predates the sixties. Booker T. Washington (April 18, 1856–November 14, 1915) left slavery and immediately pursued an education, which he saw as the way to advance black people in the United States. As a devout Christian, he focused on personal responsibility, hard work, frugality, and gaining private property. Among other accomplishments, he, along with benefactor Julius Rosenwald, built nearly five thousand schools throughout the south to improve the education of blacks.

His counterpart, W. E. B. Du Bois (February 23, 1868–August 27, 1963), believed that racism was the main problem facing blacks. He thought capitalism was the primary cause of racism. He focused on protestations against racism and using political, social justice strategies; he was one of the founders of the NAACP. "Du Bois identified as a socialist and belonged to the Socialist Party from 1910 to 1912."[51] At the age of ninety-three, he joined the communist party.

Du Bois reminds us of the long Marxian history in America, which seeks to cast every failure of black people to advance as an issue of social injustice rather than one where the socially inherited assumptions, breakdown of morality, faith, marriage, family structure (fatherlessness), devaluing education or the inaccessibility to good education (which can be overcome with some form of a voucher), a good work ethic, and personal responsibility play a vital role. Washington reminds us of how important it is to face social problems and all other problems, from a biblical position with a Christian spirit.

As Christians, we should speak out against all injustices, including unlawful death by police and the infliction of wrongful harm on the lives of innocent people and their livelihood, especially when such crimes are made to be instrumental in advocating one's position against crime. We must recognize that carrying the BLM banner while rejecting some of the immoralities of BLM does nothing to neutralize the phrase. The promoters of BLM do not care if Christians dislike some of their agenda because they will welcome anyone who will advertise their brand. And the undeniable truth is that BLM is hollow and deceptive. Their duplicity is evident in light

50. Steele, *White Guilt*, 177–78.
51. "NAACP History: W. E. B. Dubois," para. 5.

of the silence about the millions of black babies murdered annually in abortion, blacks wantonly killed by blacks, and black innocents killed by black rioters; apparently, those black lives do not matter. In a strong sense, BLM rejected Martin Luther King for Jessie Jackson and Al Sharpton.

Therefore, the banner really means only some black lives matter, which is not a banner any Christian should carry. Although Christians strongly advocate for the family, dedicated and knowledgeable parenting, we do not use the phrase "planned parenthood." The reason is simple. The term "planned parenthood" has become synonymous with the organization that promotes and profits from the execution of prenatal babies. We do not even want to be remotely associated with them or making them more well-known, and I think we should feel and act the same way towards BLM.

We should pray for the gospel to advance in this situation. We should pray for pastors and Christians in the cities of destruction as they minister Christ's truth and his love to the people. We should pray for those who have positions of influence in such tragedies to practice God's impartial justice and to speak up for Christ. We should pray for all the victims of actual injustice. In this tragedy, we should grieve for every victim of injustice, as understood by Scripture. We should, in our own sphere of influence, speak often, clearly, and Christianly.

6

Woke

What Does It Mean?

Woke, Some Background

MERRIAM-WEBSTER DICTIONARY STATES, "STAY *woke* became a watchword in parts of the black community for those who were self-aware, questioning the dominant paradigm and striving for something better. But *stay woke* and *woke* became part of a wider discussion in 2014, immediately following the shooting of Michael Brown in Ferguson, Missouri. The word *woke* became entwined with the Black Lives Matter movement; instead of just being a word that signaled awareness of injustice or racial tension, it became a word of action. Activists were *woke* and called on others to *stay woke*."[1]

Contemporarily Defined and Used

The term "woke" is now used throughout our culture and even in evangelicalism and the SBC. Being woke means having an intense awareness of injustices (as defined by social justice) that need to be fought against, repented of, atoned for, and corrected according to social justice. While social injustices primarily focus on matters of racism, social justice also includes issues such as economic and gender inequality, protecting abortion rights, homosexual rights, or transgender rights. Woke activists usually and immediately see social injustices through the lens of critical race theory or

Not Means *definition*

---

1. "Stay Woke," para. 3.

social justice, viewing these issues as oppressed (minority) vs. oppressor (majority). An unfortunate and all too prevalent characteristic of wokeness is seeing, or at least publicly presenting, nearly every obstacle to acceptance or success of a black person as due to racism when it may, at times, be as simple as not having the needed job skills, having a disrespectful attitude, appearance (as in dressing disrespectfully or as known troublemakers), or displaying a generally unpleasant personality, which are some of the same things that result in white people not being accepted by other white people and employers. Thus, it is clearly not based on race.

The evangelical white woke among us exhibit this characteristic (quickly attributing rejection of or lack of success of a black person to racism) in their public speech as frequently as they used to, before being overcome with wokeness, attribute failures to such things as the breakdown of the family, irresponsibility, laziness, or inaccessibility to or unwillingness to obtain an education in a society that demands a certain level of skills to be successful. Those referred to as woke are super sensitive to white on black crimes, although they are less sensitive to black on white crimes.

For example, those who are woke will almost instantaneously condemn the alleged perpetrator of racism and injustice while assuming the innocence of the victim before all the facts are known in an alleged white on black crime. However, they are slow to charge the black on white perpetrator with racism or criminal behavior, and many times they remain eerily silent when a black on white injustice is alleged. This missing response can apply to a host of other injustices so long as it is not white on black or majority perpetrators and minority victims. Sadly, this same wokeness is evident among *some* leaders in the SBC, which is evidenced by their consistently rapid response to condemn alleged white on black injustices (or white on minority), and noticeable silence or token mention regarding alleged black on white injustices (or minority on white).

Being woke provides a filter for interpreting Scripture to justify their social justice emphases. Even when they speak of themes such as pro-life or complementarianism, they frequently invoke elements of critical race theory and social justice. Woke Christians make explicit or implicit comments that teach if you are white, you will be a white supremacist until Christ returns. Even if you become woke, that does not necessarily remove the stain of racism or deliver you from being a white supremacist.

This inability to be wholly delivered is because whiteness is more than skin color. It is what is inherent to a white person. That is to say that

Who has said "repenting of being white"?

repenting of being white means one is repenting of his whiteness. His whiteness includes the fact that he is, as a white person, an oppressor. Consequently, he can never be genuinely delivered from his sin of being an oppressor because it is inherent in being white, whiteness.

If you oppose critical race theory (fail to support the minority for whatever reason), you are an oppressor (misogynist, sexist, racist, or bigot), or you are phobic (homophobic, transphobic, Islamophobic, xenophobic). The use of such words as in the first set is designed to shut down discussion because they presuppose you cannot have an argument for your position that does not emanate from one of these sins—especially one they want to hear; therefore, you are not the type of person that deserves a hearing. Using phobias as in the second set of words not only presupposes you cannot have an argument for your position that does not emanate from sin and prejudice, these words also taint you with having a psychological phobia (fear); therefore, you need psychiatric help rather than an answer to your racist objection.

Our first response should be to reject such labels and that we fear these people. Then we should give biblical reasons why we reject such labels and why we hold the opinion we do. Their name-calling tactics are cowardly and uncivil approaches but not to the degree of those who scream obscenities at you so that you cannot speak or become unwilling to talk. But, they all have the same purpose of intimidation through insult as opposed to civil and intellectual dialogue. It is worth noting, their forefather, Karl Marx, seems to have set the standard. In characterizing Marx, the young radical German revolutionary, Carl Schurz, said, "To no opinion which differed from his own did he accord the honor of even a condescending consideration . . . Everyone who contradicted him, he treated with abject contempt."[2]

Even issues that do not actually fall into one of the categories mentioned are treated as though they do, which permits the social justice group to shut down any discussion they choose to avoid. They know full well that many whites will go silent rather than be labeled a racist—white guilt. For the woke, almost all social issues are seen through social justice, critical race the nd intersectionality, which elevates the place of racism in the discussion, even when it does not fit at all.[3]

---

2. Schurz et al., *Reminiscences of Carl Schurz*, 188–89.

3. I use the term "woke" to include those who may not claim that title for themselves, but upon examination, they often speak consistently or reflectively of being woke.

For example, on the eve of January 24, 2020, March for Life, Dr. Russell Moore, president of the Ethics and Religious Liberty Commission of the SBC, tweeted a link to an article, which originated as a podcast on April 20, 2018. That is to say, on the eve of the sanctity of human life day, Moore felt compelled to post an article he had written almost two years prior addressing issues of healthcare, affirmative action, black lives matter, and immigration along with the issue of abortion.

I believe Moore's action misuses the pro-life position of defining life as sacred from conception to natural death in order to elevate other social issues about which he is passionate. Whether he deems his actions as a misuse, I will leave between him and God. I see it as a misuse because it diminishes the uniquely significant place of fighting against the prenatal extermination of babies. While it is true that as Christians, we are pro-sanctity of life at all stages and in all circumstances, we should not consider them all equal in their unbridled and barbaric lethality. Therefore, we should not use the pro-life march to showcase other issues that are not close to the inherent lethality of abortion, infanticide, and euthanasia.

"[The Pro-life march was] founded by anti-abortion activist and Roman Catholic convert Nellie Gray in 1974 to protest the one-year anniversary of the Supreme Court's decision to legalize abortion nationwide in *Roe v. Wade*."[4] The march was established to protest the legalization of abortion. The founders believed it would be a one-time event because they believed the Supreme Court would overturn their decision. Since the decision has not been reversed, the march has continued to highlight this assault on prenatal human life for forty-six years. Dr. Moore's mingling of other social issues on the occasion of this march unnecessarily promotes different social agendas while diminishing the atrocity of abortion. I believe this was an unintended consequence of his decision. Nevertheless, his actions grant liberals who seek open borders, support various forms of amnesty, affirmative action, or support matters that relate to prison reform and poverty, to equate these issues with the tragedy of the devilish abortion of babies.

His unguarded mixing of these topics gives evangelical liberals, or even those who are not Christian, a means to recognize someone as pro-life without the person being against the prenatal murder of babies, something they will gladly use. For example, regarding the coronavirus, Joe Biden tweeted, "Let me be very clear: No one is expendable. No matter your age, race, gender, religion, ethnicity, sexual orientation, or disability. No life

4. Burton, "March for Life." See also Memmott, "Nellie Gray Dies."

is worth losing to add one more point to the Dow."[5] Then, SBC Pastor Dwight McKissic included Biden's words in his tweet, saying, "You would think this would be the position of the Republican candidate for president. Discovering that pro-birth does not necessarily mean pro-life. Biden has adopted the pro-life position with regard to placing the value of vulnerable lives over the economy."[6]

Joe Biden is a long-time supporter of Roe vs. Wade's legalization of abortion, although he has vacillated on certain things like federal funding of abortion. According to David Siders, Biden said, in his speech at a Planned Parenthood Clinic, "He would support codifying *Roe* as defined by a later decision that affirmed the landmark case's central principles. 'It should be the law,' Biden said."[7] Even though Biden supports the vile murder of babies, Pastor McKissic feels no shame in mischaracterizing President Trump's position and reducing his pro-life position to pro-birth while using "pro-life" as a descriptive of a pro-abortionist. This is the dreadful blurring of lines between words and meanings to advance a personal agenda. I suspect we will see more of the same kind of scandalous absurdities.

Maintaining a guarded and absolute distinction between abortion and infanticide and problems such as illegal immigration or affirmative action is essential, and doing so does not mean that such concerns are unimportant or are not pro-life issues, generally speaking. For example, the American Cancer Society focuses its energy and resources on only one sickness, and that is cancer. There are many sicknesses, but the American Cancer Society researches and treats only cancer. This singular focus stands out in their name. They do not practice heart surgery, podiatry, treat broken legs, the flu, or aches and pains not related to cancer. But that does not mean they do not deem other diseases as significant.

Another example could be seen at church. A friend tells me he has the flu (the typical winter variety). I genuinely feel sorry for him, and I say so as I back away from him. Then, I turn and walk further down the hall, and I run into Mary. Mary tells me she has been diagnosed with cancer. I do not say to her, yeah, Bob just told me he has the flu. I hate that you're both

5. Biden, "Let Me Be Very Clear." I believe this was an unwarranted besmirching of President Trump's handling of the COVID-19 virus in which he considers both the virus and potential devastation to people that will happen if the economy collapses; I would argue this is precisely what leaders should consider if they care about the citizenry.

6. See McKissic, "You Would Think."

7. Siders, "Biden Calls for Enshrining Roe v. Wade," paras. 2–3. See also Kaczynski, "Biden Described Being an 'Odd Man Out.'"

sick. No one would even consider such a comparison even though both are sicknesses. And both can be lethal, but that is as far as the comparison goes; therefore, be on guard. While all are created in the image of God, not all areas someone might be concerned about in which being created in the image of God is relevant are as significant as abortion. We should include infanticide, but not border control, affirmative action, or healthcare because infanticide, like abortion, is barbarically and systematically lethal. Moreover, the fact is that we could end abortion in America tomorrow if the Democratic party would denounce it as the inhumane, ghastly savagery that it is.

Biblical Evaluation of Wokeness

Biblically, we are to see all things through the lens of Scripture by the illumination of the Holy Spirit (1 John 2:27) and Christ, who is the Truth (John 17:17). We are not to see life through the lens of the oppressed and oppressor, racism, humanly defined social justice, or through the lens of wokeness, which seeks to invoke the issue of race in almost every discussion. Biblically, black liberation theology, feminist theology, homosexual theology, or any other humanly constructed lenses, including social justice, critical race theory, and intersectionality, is neither necessary nor beneficial to interpreting Scripture or to biblically and accurately addressing cultural problems. They only enable the interpreter to arrive at the conclusion he is seeking, which is not the authorial intent of the writer—God.[8] The historical/grammatical method transcends such matters as time, race, sex, and culture because it asks, based on the history, grammar, and context at the time of the biblical event, what the author intended by what he said and how the original recipients understood it.

One's experience might help to expand various applications of Scripture, but the interpretation is tied to authorial intent. Scripture emphasizes God's justice, which is impartial justice (Rom 2:11; Eph 6:9; Col 3:25), and so should his followers (Jas 2:1–5), whereas critical race theory and wokeness emphasize social justice—socialistic justice. In contrast to social justice, which shows partiality, is racially or minority biased, unequally applied through immoral and external group-driven merit and accountability, God's justice is equal and impartial. It is equal in that every person

8. This is the correct approach to the Scripture, which is arrived at through the process of the Grammatical-Historical Method of interpretation.

is judged by the same standard, unlike social justice. It is impartial in that it is applied in the same way to everyone irrespective of race, sex, or any other human distinction such as skin color or whether one is a part of the minority or majority. God's justice is holy and righteous because it is based on who he is in contrast to social justice, which is based upon arbitrary, humanly devised external standards.

Consequently, a singular focus on pro-life to mean and require actively opposing abortion (and other practices with immediate and absolute lethality such as infanticide or even euthanasia) does not imply we are not pro-life in other life-focus areas any more than the National Cancer Society's singular focus on cancer means they are not supportive of wellness in all areas. That would be true only if they were against the promotion of health in other areas. Similarly, it would only be true of those of us who advocate a supreme focus on abortion, infanticide, and euthanasia if we were against supporting the sanctity of human life in other areas where it is relevant. Lastly, our disagreement on what should be included in those areas (such as border control, affirmative action, and minimum wage) and how they should be managed does not equal failing to be pro-life, as would be the case if someone is not against abortion.

7

The Woke and the SBC's Massive Problem
of White Supremacy

Southeastern Baptist Theological Seminary and Southern Baptist Theological Seminary (SEBTS and SBTS, respectively) seem to be the most woke of our six seminaries in the SBC. I am not aware of any such concerns about the other four seminaries.[1] Even at SEBTS and SBTS, I am not claiming that many professors are involved. I am not aware of evidence that indicates there are more than a small minority. But these two seminaries appear to have the most leaders who are vocal in speaking supportively of various aspects of critical race theory, social justice, and intersectionality, or at least they often speak consistently with them.[2] Racism, according to critical race theory, is a category of "sin" that applies to only one group (white people), and if you are in that group, you can never fully repent, be forgiven of, and be delivered from racism.

Some Southern Baptists have claimed that there is no evidence of leaders using, supporting, or promoting critical race theory in the SBC. They say the claim that some do is false and the result of the Conservative

1. This is not a denial of a more pervasive problem. I am only dealing with what I know.

2. To hear SEBTS professors who speak favorably or hospitably of CRT and Black Liberation Theology at SEBTS, listen to http://www.worldviewconversation.com/. For professors who reflect CRT language at SBTS listen to Thenewcalvinist, "Stain of Mohler 3." For a survey of the problem in the SBC watch By What Standard, see https://founders.org/cinedoc/. You may find these resources in Appendix 5 or on my blog: Rogers, "Trouble in the SBC." Additionally, if no one uses or endorses critical race theory, then why the need for Resolution 9?

Baptist Network's (CBN) misrepresentation of the SBC.[3] For the record, here are two. In the book, *Removing the Stain of Racism from the Southern Baptist Convention,* Dr. Jarvis Williams says, "Southern Baptists should be quick to listen and slow to speak on race when they do not understand the issues. White supremacy and racism are complicated issues. These issues relate to concepts such as racialization, *critical race theory,* mass incarceration, economic inequality, educational inequality, and other forms of systemic injustice"[4] (italics added). It is also worth noting that he categorizes all of these as resulting from "systemic injustice." Instead of stating that they may be due, at least in part, to other non-justice or nonracial factors such as systemic fatherlessness, out-of-wedlock marriage, devaluing education, lack of emphasis on personal responsibility, familial culture, and inherited assumptions; he is satisfied to *only* blame racial injustice, which is characteristic of critical race theory. In his chapter, Dr. Curtis A. Woods says of Jarvis Williams, "He writes and speaks consistently on race and theology in multiple venues. Williams's chapter incorporates history, sociology, *critical race theory,* and New Testament scholarship into a candid conversation about the myth of modern racial reasoning"[5] (italics added). Thus, the rebuttal to the concerns about the CBN is without merit.

The most significant conservative evangelical statement on these issues is *The Statement on Social Justice & the Gospel.*[6] Interestingly, Dr. Albert Mohler would not join men like John MacArthur, Tom Ascol, Voddie Baucham, Justin Peters, Craig Mitchell, and over 14,000 others who signed the statement.[7] I am a signer as well. Mohler seemed to become upset when probed about not signing the statement at the 2019 Shepherd's Conference. He said, "It is not pride of authorship, but I am just reluctant to sign onto anything that is not creedal and confessional that doesn't express exactly how I want to say something."[8]

3. I have seen these kinds of statements on social media and interacted with a few. I have a copy of one person's words to this effect. I do not feel the need to disclose the person's name since the name is not essential to highlight the charge. I assume many others have heard the same.

4. Williams, "Biblical Steps Toward Removing the Stain," 45.

5. Woods, "Are We There Yet?," 123.

6. See the Statement on Social Justice and the Gospel at https://statementonsocialjustice.com/. For comments on the statement, see Roach, "Social Justice Statement."

7. As of January 11, 2021, there were 15,792 signers.

8. Smith, "Al Mohler Explains," para. 13.

Now, I understand being uncomfortable with signing a statement that you did not have a part in drafting because it will not communicate your beliefs as precisely as if you were a contributor—participating in the "authorship"; the same is also true of creeds and confessions of faith. I think most might have the same reluctance. But even if a person is a contributor to a statement that has multiple authors, it is highly unlikely that the wording will be "exactly" what any one of them would have said had it been a single author endeavor; to wit, it will not satisfy Mohler's criterion to "express exactly how I want to say something." This is true of statements, confessions, and creeds as well.

Consequently, if we all took the position of Dr. Mohler, it is unlikely that anyone, or at least very few, could sign any document that expresses the view of a group. If no one signs statements, unless Mohler's criterion of being a contributor, or communicating "exactly" how each person wants to say something, statements like *The Statement on Social Justice and the Gospel* or the *Nashville Statement*, A Coalition for Biblical Sexuality (the latter Mohler did sign, along with over twenty-four thousand other people) could not exist. If Mohler's criterion must be met, there will be few endorsers of statements like *The Danvers Statement* on biblical manhood and womanhood. There will rarely, if ever, be collective statements encompassing the positions of conservative Christianity on vital matters of the day.

These statements not only help to state the position of the authors and those who sign on later; they also have a tutorial component of teaching others. Additionally, Dr. Mohler appears to have signed statements he did not help draft, as noted in the article cited in the following footnote.[9] While the Baptist Faith and Message 2000 is confessional, he did vigorously seek to persuade others to accept his preferred wording and condition of being a contributor.[10] Although I initially found Mohler's reason for not signing *The Statement on Social Justice* to be unconvincing, I accepted it as fact. At the time, I was unaware of any indication that he might be sympathetic to aspects of the social justice movement that are not supported in *The Statement on Social Justice*. I now think there are indications of just that.

9. Baptist Press Staff, "Southern Baptist Leaders Issue Joint Statement." Mohler is not listed as a contributor. I suppose it is possible that it expressed his position precisely as he would have said it.

10. Although this is a confession, I contend that his use of this as a reason for not signing is now seen to not be the most precise reason he did not sign *The Statement on Social Justice*.

It seems Dr. Mohler did not sign because he disagrees with some of the statement's declarations, as he interprets them.[11] For example, Mohler disagrees with *The Statement on Social Justice's* declaration, "We reject any teaching that encourages racial groups to view themselves as privileged oppressors or entitled victims of oppression. While we are to weep with those who weep, we deny that a person's feelings of offense or oppression necessarily prove that someone else is guilty of sinful behaviors, oppression, or prejudice."

Mohler disagreed with this statement in his chapel message to students at SBTS, saying, "There are victims right now of social forces of oppression" and "Just because those on the radical left point to everything as oppression doesn't mean that nothing is oppression."[12] It appears, for whatever reason, that Mohler seems to have inferred something that I would say is neither explicitly nor implicitly present in *The Statement on Social Justice.*

The first quote in *The Statement on Social Justice* to which Mohler refers is an explicit rejection of social justice teachings; social justice is the context of the statement. It says, "We reject any teaching that encourages racial groups to view themselves as privileged oppressors or entitled victims of oppression."[13] This statement is a concise and precise rejection of critical race theory and cultural Marxism. Cultural Marxism emphasizes group identity and responsibility to the point that it replaces individual identity and responsibility. It promotes conflict between the oppressed group (black minorities particularly) and the oppressor group (white majorities particularly). A person's identity and responsibility are not based on the individual's actions but the actions of the group, thereby making all the individuals in the oppressor group guilty, and all individuals in the oppressed group victims, even individuals in the group who did not participate. The statement says explicitly, "We reject any teaching that encourages racial groups." They are not rejecting that someone could be oppressed or an oppressor. Instead, they reject *the teaching* that promotes racial group identity as privileged or entitled victims; thus, they reject cultural Marxism. Therefore, *The*

11. Briggs, "Why Al Mohler Didn't Sign." See also Roach, "Social Justice Statement."

12. Mohler also specifically attributes his unwillingness to sign the social justice statement to his disagreement with some of the content, saying, "But I could not sign the statement because of some particular areas." PJ Tibayan, "Albert Mohler on Social Justice and the Gospel," 15:13–16; 15:19–25. See also Briggs, "Why Al Mohler Didn't Sign," 11:01–15.

13. See the Statement on Social Justice and the Gospel at https://statementonsocialjustice.com/, esp. §12.

Statement on Social Justice is not a denial of every kind of oppression or entitled group possible in any scenario, as Dr. Mohler seems to understand it, which appears to be reading into the statement more than is there.[14] Instead, it is a rejection of the social justice idea that one's racial group identity determines whether someone is an oppressor or the oppressed. However, Mohler may, in fact, disagree with the statement's disavowal of the legitimacy of social justice. I will leave that between him and God.

The second statement in *The Statement on Social Justice* is an explicit denial that a "person's *feelings* of offense . . . *necessarily prove* that someone is guilty of sinful behaviors, oppression, or prejudices" (italics added). To Mohler's criticism, the declaration is not a denial that some have been or are oppressed, but rather only that "feelings of offense . . . [do] not prove . . . guilt" of others. To further demonstrate Mohler's understanding is not reflective of the author's views, you may read John MacArthur's articles on social justice on Grace To You's website and listen to his four-part series on the subject on YouTube.[15] None of these support Dr. Mohler's conclusions. See also *By What Standard* by Tom Ascol.[16]

I also find it interesting that Dr. Mohler has chosen to publicly defend the woke among us, such as Dr. Jarvis Williams, Dr. Matthew Hall, Dr. Curtis Woods, and Dr. Danny Aiken (who appears to be at least friendly towards wokeness and approving of *some* problematic professors and their teaching at SEBTS).[17] Yet, he remains silent when un-woke notables, like Dr. John MacArthur, Dr. Paige Patterson, Dr. Tom Ascol, or a host of others, come under attack. The day after the launch of the Conservative Baptist Network, Dr. Mohler tweeted, unprovoked, the following derogatory remark, "The real network of Southern Baptists is called the Southern Baptist Convention. It's going to meet June 9–10 in Orlando. I look forward to joining you there."[18]

In response, Rod D. Martin, one of the founders of the Conservative Baptist Network tweeted, "With great respect, Al, a lot of us are noticing the difference between your response time to the launch of a group of Baptist Faith and Message 2000 supportive Baptists and your response time to a

14. Entitled groups not included in the statement could be employees who were promised pay for their work or retirees who paid into a retirement program.

15. Search Social Justice at https://www.gty.org/.

16. Ascol, "By What Standard."

17. This is not to imply there are not a host of first-class orthodox scholars at SEBTS.

18. Mohler, "Real Network of Southern Baptists."

woman 'teaching pastor' at the SBCPC"[19] (Southern Baptist Convention Pastor's Conference). Dr. Mohler later said he was not trying to be condescending. All those I have heard from that are associated with the CBN don't seem convinced, myself included. The number of likes by those who oppose the CBN appears to reflect the same perspective as the CBN does on Mohler's clarification.

Then there is the jointly authored book by Dr. Mohler, Dr. Curtis Woods, Dr. Jarvis Williams, and Dr. Mathew Hall, *Removing the Stain of Racism from the Southern Baptist Convention*. The book was the brainchild of Dr. Kevin Jones, who is a professor at Boyce College at SBTS.[20] All of them are employed at SBTS or its college, Boyce. It appears that Dr. Mohler may have coined the phrase "the stain of racism."[21] While I find some commendable ideas in the book, I also find some deeply troubling ideas, one of which I will address in chapter 13.

Many people who are supportive of the Me-Too Movement, both inside and outside the SBC and the *Houston Chronicle*, portrayed the SBC as infested with sexual abusers, which goes unchecked because of self-serving leaders who will not address them and even hide such atrocities.[22]

Similarly, Dr. Mohler portrays the culture and church, including the SBC, as having a "massive" racism problem, and this is one-way white racism toward blacks. He emphatically states, "I can't associate with any assertion that we do not *have* a *massive problem* in the society and in the church *with claims of racial superiority* and with historic patterns of claims of white racial superiority and with the fact that remnants and ongoing manifestations of *those claims of white racial superiority continue*"[23] (italics added).

19. See Martin's reply, "With Great Respect."

20. There are other contributors as well.

21. Thenewcalvinist, "Stain," 15:59–16:29.

22. Listen to my message series, "In Defense of God's Order and the Gospel." This is not to make light of those who have been tragically abused. Nor is it to say that abuses and cover-ups have not happened. Instead, it is to state there were also many who were misrepresented and hurt by the Chronicle's coverage and the trial by internet, which distorted many situations. See also my article, "Right and Wrong."

23. Thenewcalvinist, "Stain." It should be noted that Dr. Mohler claims to strongly reject cultural Marxism, but what I am pointing out is that he speaks and uses terminology that is consistent with critical race theory and simultaneously inconsistent with Scripture. He has hired faculty like Professor Curtis Woods (chairman of the Resolutions Committee that presented Resolution 9), Jarvis Williams, and Matthew Hall, who reflect ideas from critical race theory and utilize it as well. My point is that Southern Seminary

Historically, I agree that some, and at times *many*, made "claims of white racial superiority" both in culture and the SBC. Currently, I assume there are *some* still making "claims of white racial superiority" in the SBC, although I do not personally have evidence of such. It seems plausible in an organization of almost sixteen million that there would be some. But to declare we "*have* a massive problem . . . in the church . . . with claims of racial superiority," as Dr. Mohler does seem unjustified, at least by the evidence he put forth. Where are the statistics and evidence that demonstrate that assumption? Where is the host of such claims by Southern Baptist members who declare they believe in "white racial superiority" that reflect the "massive problem" of which he speaks?[24]

While I know some cultish people believe in white supremacy, I must say I have never met a Southern Baptist in my thirty-six years of pastoring Southern Baptist churches that *said or claimed* to believe such an idea. It seems if there were a "massive problem," I might have seen many or at least some since I have pastored in Arkansas and Oklahoma and served on staff in Texas. My experience is not a denial of the existence of such people, and it is surely not a denial of unspoken racism in the SBC. Instead, it is, without irrefutable evidence, a rejection of the *claims of racial superiority* being a "massive problem" in the SBC. I have met a few people during my years of pastoring that I deem, by their words and behavior, that they are racists, but even they did not declare a belief in white racial superiority. And that is what he says is precisely a "massive problem" in the church—SBC.[25]

My rejection of the unsubstantiated massiveness of the problem of racism is not, in any way, to be interpreted as a denial that racism exists. In some places, it seems more prevalent. Further, I believe all genuine racism is sin. Even if you have seen or met some racists in the SBC, ask yourself if your experience rises numerically to a "massive problem" given all the Southern Baptists, you know? The SBC has over forty-seven thousand churches, 14,813,234 members, and 5,297,778 in weekly attendance.[26]

---

has faculty who embrace critical race theory at various levels and speak and research consistently with it.

24. If he relies on people who embrace critical race theory, I will not count their philosophically deduced definition of white supremacy as credible.

25. I assume he includes the SBC in the word "church" since that is the ecclesiastical body to which he, SBTS, and the vast majority of the people to whom he is speaking belong.

26. See "Fast Facts about the SBC," table 1.

While Dr. Mohler's claim does not seem to comport with objective evidence, it is consistent with the perennial claim of critical race theory.

It is clear that Dr. Mohler and others do not use the word "stain" to speak merely of something that happened and left a mark or blemish, a past act or time that ended. This conclusion is evident in their statements and even more apparent in their book itself.[27] Instead, the word speaks of something ongoing. If it were a historical statement only, it would be referenced in the past tense rather than a present tense indicating something that is unforgiven, and therefore unresolved.

My comments have nothing to do with liking, respecting, and appreciating Dr. Mohler. I supported him when he was inaugurated as president of SBTS, and I have continued to do so over the years. It is only in recent years that I have become troubled by *some* things he has said or done, particularly with regard to homosexuality and critical race theory.[28] Thus, my concerns are not reflective of the mentality of an all-out battle against Dr. Mohler. Instead, my comments reflect my concerns about the direction of the SBC generally and where Dr. Mohler positions himself specifically, which seems to be more inconsistent lately. Or I could say, more consistently demonstrating sympathy with wokeness, mildly accommodating homosexuality, and even against or unsupportive of those of us who have concerns, as voiced by the CBN. I do want to mention that Dr. Mohler has, at times, been very forthright in condemning critical race theory.[29] However, an inconsistency among the woke or those sympathetic to it is not unusual.

Although I will speak to Resolution 9 in chapter 9, I must now mention that Dr. Mohler did write negatively about the contents of Resolution 9 in his briefing on June 14, 2019. Since the Resolution had passed and the convention was over, it harvested little or no lasting effect.[30] Mohler attended the SBC convention that passed Resolution 9, and he chose to remain silent when his comments would have been significant, maybe even enough to have stopped the adoption of Resolution 9. Or at least Tom Ascol's amendment probably would have passed.

27. Williams and Jones, *Removing the Stain.*

28. His change regarding homosexuality relates to his repentance over his previous rejection of the concept of sexual orientation. I have written an article that critiques his change and his defense of his change. Although, to date, I have not posted it. I plan to in the future at ronniewrogers.com.

29. Thenewcalvinist, "Stain."

30. Mohler, "Briefing."

In light of the continued sizable and vocal disapproval of Resolution 9, the Resolutions Committee sought to defend further and clarify why they presented it. And how, if understood correctly, it was not a problem. While their explanation did not resolve the issues many of us have with the Resolution, Mohler tweeted positively about the committee's communication. He tweeted, "I appreciate @baptistpress & members of the 2019 Resolutions Committee talking here about Res 9. This is the right tone. I am sure it is released in good faith."[31] Once again, Dr. Mohler quickly took his stand with the woke and against those who were troubled by the social justice presence in the SBC.

In summary, consider the following: Dr. Mohler's assessment that the SBC has a "massive problem" with people making "claims of white racial superiority" is consistent with critical race theory, but, to my knowledge, it has not been demonstrated to be compatible with evidential reality. Where is the evidence? Dr. Mohler is unwilling to sign the statement on social justice. He is quick to support colleagues who are woke and under attack but withholds similar support from those who are not woke when they are attacked. He tweets negatively about the CBN, a conservative national organization with goals paralleling the heart of the Conservative Resurgence, of which Dr. Mohler was a participant. He speaks supportively of the committee defending Resolution 9. In contrast, he did not agree with those who question the Resolution, at least not enough to have spoken against the Resolution at the convention when it mattered.[32] I conclude he is sympathetic with the woke on social justice, whereas he is not with those who oppose social justice.

It is crucial to keep in mind that arguably the most glaring indicator of the nature of Resolution 9, and thereby the plan of at least some on the Resolution Committee, came when we learned of the original resolution on critical race theory, which was written by Stephen Michael Feinstein. His Resolution called for removing critical race theory and intersectionality from our institutions and churches.[33] The committee rejected his proposal and instead crafted a resolution that supported the use of these Marxist concepts as analytical tools. Their rejection of a resolution calling for the

31. Mohler, "Southern Baptists Are Up to the Challenge."

32. He now says he does not think it was a good idea for the Resolution Committee to have presented Resolution 9. As of June 2020, he has made statements to this effect. That being said does not in and of itself mean that he now disagrees with the resolution, although he may.

33. See Chapter 9 and Appendix 4.

removal of these theories, as well as their acceptance of them as useful analytical tools, is indicative of a favorable attitude toward critical race theory and intersectionality.

8

The Inadequacy of Repentance in Critical Race Theory's Racism

Critical Race Theory's Impotent Forgiveness

Dr. Jarvis Williams has been the Associate Professor of New Testament Interpretation at SBTS since 2013. He said, "The stain of racism *exists* in the SBC because of the enduring effects of white supremacist thinking . . . by their insensitive responses to incontrovertible examples of racial injustice in the US"[1] (italics added). As mentioned, the stain of racism is not exhausted by references to something in the past but as something that continues today. Notice the present tense of "*exists* . . . enduring . . . [and] thinking."[2]

Dr. Matthew J. Hall was appointed as provost and senior vice president for the academic administration of The Southern Baptist Theological Seminary in April 2019. He said, "I am a racist . . . *I'm going to struggle with racism and white supremacy until the day I die and get my glorified body*"[3] (italics added). Such a statement is not derived from Scripture but is absolutely consistent with and reflective of critical race theory.

In light of Scripture, we should always make clear that whatever we repent of in seeking forgiveness from God is wholly dealt with spiritually

---

1. Thenewcalvinist, "Stain," 43:00–43:11; 43:31–39.

2. This understanding is explicitly attested to throughout the book *Removing the Stain of Racism from the Southern Baptist Convention*.

3. For the New Christian Intellectual, "I Am a Racist," 0:18–19, 0:30–35.

A Corruption of Consequence

(Matt 12:41; Luke 15:7; 17:3; John 3:3; Rom 6:6, 16–19; 1 Cor 6:11; Gal 5:18; Eph 1:1–5; Titus 3:3–7; 1 Pet 1:13–16; 4:2; 1 John 1:9). We are delivered from the power of sin to enslave us. It does not continue to exist in a person's life as something that requires further repentance, forgiveness, or acknowledgment of its presence unless the person chooses to continue to repeat the sin. While people could have done something in the past that left a mark on their life, it is not still active. It existed, but it does not always exist. However, the sin of critical race theory's racism knows no power of repentance and victory by obedience to Christ in this life.[4] Dr. Hall's words are characteristic of critical race theory and not Scripture. After Hall was called out on his racist statement, he spoke differently about racism in a later article.[5] Inconsistency is not uncommon among the woke in the SBC, particularly when there is pushback.

4. The stain of racism existing in the SBC and using white supremacy and privilege (an ill-gotten privilege gained by systemic white supremacy) permeate their speaking and writing that I have seen on this subject with little if any mention of God's great forgiveness and deliverance for such in response to our repentance and faith.

5. He has written subsequently in an article subtitled, "Only the Gospel of Christ Can Solve the Problem of Racism. Only the Gospel Can Assure Us That in Christ There Is Hope for Reconciliation with God, and with One Another." He says, "At its core, racism is about the sin of partiality. It imposes a double standard on one group of human beings on the basis of perceived physical characteristics. The Bible is clear that God shows no partiality and he expects his people to reflect his character (for example, Deut 10:17; Deut 16:19; Prov 24:23; Rom 2:11) . . . But let's be very clear: Christian witness must reject CRT and the ideological foundations that shape it, along with the proposals it offers for change . . . CRT assumes a basic materialism, ignoring spiritual realities and, in particular, the truth that human beings are made in the image of God . . . Because of its deficiencies, CRT can never adequately diagnose the fundamental problems inherent in racism, nor can it adequately prescribe a true solution. Only the gospel of Christ can do that . . . While the biblical worldview certainly acknowledges injustice in a fallen world, the defining story of Scripture is redemptive, centered on the person and work of Christ, propelling history forward to the glory of God. This story is inseparable from the miracle of the new birth and the necessity of personal saving faith in Jesus as Lord and Savior." Hall, "For He Is Our Peace," paras. 5, 7.

Notice that he does not denounce his claim to being a hopeless racist in this life. If he were going to denounce critical race theory fully, indeed, he should denounce his claim, which is dependent on the integrity of critical race theory because his statement did not come from Scripture. To my knowledge, he has not repudiated his statement that he is a racist, but even if he has, it remains a statement drawn from beyond the Scripture. Additionally, it is common for the woke to reject the materialistic nature of cultural Marxism, but that is not its only problem. The woke are continually talking about the sin of racism (as Hall did in his original quote and here), but, quite unbiblically, they frequently fail to declare the availability of immediate forgiveness for that sin upon repentance and faith in Christ (something that Hall's explanation omits). That is characteristic of critical

Dr. Curtis Woods joined the SBTS faculty in 2018 as the Assistant Professor of Applied Theology and Biblical Spirituality.[6] Dr. Woods wrote a chapter in the book *Removing the Stain of Racism in the Southern Baptist Convention*. He answered the question of whether "we are there yet," meaning have we overcome racism, saying, "As a brother, I will answer with a prayerful, patient, and positive tone. No, we have not arrived. Christ has not set up his kingdom on earth. May Southern Baptists keep walking and working together to remove the stain of racism from the SBC until he comes! Maranatha!"[7]

Similarly, on a panel discussion, Woods said, "Biblical theology and eschatology tell us that we will *not remove the stain* until Christ comes back and sets up his coming kingdom"[8] (italics added). He answers that the Bible tells us not even Christ can remove the stain of racism in the life of white people, regardless of how many times they repent. Such sentiments are consistent with critical race theory's racism. This sin is the sin of white supremacy.

White people suffer from this sin because of their skin pigmentation and because they benefit from being white. That is to say, their whiteness, which includes skin color, is not limited to it. Critical race theory declares white supremacy is systemic, institutional racism. The charge of white supremacy is true even if a white person opposes all genuine racism. And if a white person did commit the sin of racism and later repent, that repentance and resulting forgiveness in Christ is not sufficient to remove the racism (white supremacy) from his life. He will need to repent again and again and even repent for the sin of other people because he shares their skin color. It is hard to imagine something more contrary to God's grace gospel than that (Luke 17:4; 24:47; Acts 2:38; 3:13; 10:43; 2 Cor 7:10; 2 Pet 3:9; Rev 2:22).

Dr. Mohler, speaking of racism as a stain, says it is exactly the right word. "It's a stain that we're going to carry as a denomination forever, till Jesus comes. But it's a stain that if we deal with rightly can actually show the

race theory, but not the gospel. Moreover, earlier I demonstrated Williams's and Woods's support of critical race theory by their own words. A fortiori, if critical race theory is to be rejected by Christians, why the need for Resolution 9?

6. As of 9/28/20, Dr. Curtis Woods accepted the call as Lead Pastor of Severns Valley Baptist Church, Elizabeth Town, KY. As of today, it is uncertain whether this entails him leaving his position at SBTS. http://kentuckytoday.staging.communityq.com/stories/woods-called-to-lead-pastor-of-severns-valley-in-etown,28204, accessed 9/28/20.

7. Woods, "Are We There Yet?," 129.

8. Thenewcalvinist, "Stain," 27:19–26.

power of Christ. And that's what I'm praying for, praying with you brothers for"[9] (italics added). Notice how we deal with the stain: "we are going to have to carry . . . forever." A present and unending situation. If it were a stain referring to the past, we could thank God for victory and forgiveness granted to us in repentance and faith, thereby highlighting the glory of God and move on. But stain is not merely a historical word. Speaking of the stain, he also says, "If we deal with it rightly, [the stain] can . . . show the power of Christ." It is obvious we have not dealt with it since he says, "if we deal with it" and "that is what I am praying for." Concerning our sin, it is the most glorious display of Christ's power in that he paid for all our sins, and God will forgive us when we exercise child-like faith in Jesus (John 3:16; Rom 10:4, 9–10).

Again, where is the biblical finality of God dealing with our sins when we repent and believe in Scripture's repeated statements and emphasis? Scripture is clear, "Come now, and let us reason together," says the Lord, "Though your sins are as scarlet, They will be as white as snow; Though they are red like crimson, They will be like wool" (Isa 1:18). Again, Isaiah says, "I, even I, am the one who wipes out your transgressions for My own sake, And I will not remember your sins" (Isa 43:25). In salvation, a Christian can live as a new creation, which each Christian is (2 Cor 5:17). We can live lives of holiness because Christians are born again, the Holy Spirit lives in us, and our slavery to sin has been defeated (Matt 12:41; Luke 15:7; 17:3; John 3:3; Rom 6:6, 16–19; 1 Cor 6:11; Gal 5:18; Eph 1:1–5; Titus 3:3–7; 1 Pet 1:13–16; 4:2; 1 John 1:9). That is why God can command us to live holy lives (1 Pet 1:15–16).

The words of Dr. Hall, Dr. Woods, and Dr. Mohler seem to have more in common with Robin DiAngelo than Isaiah. DiAngelo says, "'Less racist' is not a fixed location based on good intentions, self-image, or past actions. It is continually strived for through on-going and demonstrated practice, and ultimately determined by peoples of Color."[10] Resultantly, neither the white individual nor God can say a person is not a racist; only other people "of color" have that power. Reemphasizing a person's inability to be freed from racism, DiAngelo also says, "Racism must be continually identified, analyzed, and challenged; *no one is ever done*"[11] (italics added).

9. Thenewcalvinist, "Stain," 47:45–48:02.

10. DiAngelo, "Anti-Racism Handout."

11. DiAngelo, "Anti-Racism Handout."

Thus, Dr. Mohler, Dr. Hall, and Dr. Woods' concept of racism, stain, does not refer to something that happened in the past, nor can it ever be in a person who repented or in the SBC, which I am quite sure DiAngelo would concur even if Scripture does not. If it were viewed as something that could be repented of, and therefore a part of the past, I would agree, but it is not, and apparently cannot be. Consequently, it appears that a white individual or the SBC cannot move beyond racism, regardless if we repent or how many times we repent. That is consistent with critical race theory but not the gospel. Moreover, it seems the SBC cannot be considered a non-racist organization so long as there are any racists among us, or if we honor anyone for anything that one time approved of slavery. Even if we categorically reject slavery and racism, biblically speaking.

According to critical race theory, there is no complete forgiveness because there will always be some racists, but also because white people are racists, and white people remain white after they repent or confess Christ. They cannot be delivered from their whiteness, their racist DNA. It is crucial to note that while they repeatedly speak about racism, "the stain," or white supremacy being with us until the end, they do not commensurately talk of effectual repentance, the incredible forgiveness in Christ, and being able to live faithfully for Christ and not be a white supremacist, which I would think would be loudly repeated if they were driven by Scripture and, therefore, referring to real racism.

Think about it this way. The sin of abortion is a personal sin for those who provide it, condone it, or receive an abortion. If abortion is against the law in America and due diligence to stop it is practiced, then there is not a present national sin; only the individuals who support abortion are sinning. Nor is every American guilty of supporting abortion (being a pro-abortionist) because they share the same skin color as those who have abortions, live in the same country, or benefit in some way from the illegal abortion industry. If someone did at one time support the abortion industry in some way, and they repented in Christ, they are fully forgiven; therefore, they are no longer a pro-abortionist.

If America then legalized abortion so that the illegal personal sin becomes legal, not only does the personal sin exist but a national sin as well. But legalization does not ipso facto make every American citizen guilty of supporting abortion or being an abortionist. We can say America is guilty, while not every American is guilty of the sin of abortion.

Then if abortion was outlawed again, the nation could repent of its prior legalization of abortion, turn from its sin, and no longer be guilty of the ongoing stain of abortion. It would once again be a personal sin, in which a person is blameworthy only if he still supports its legalization or, in some way, supports it as an illegal institution. Imagine calling someone pro-abortion who was against abortion, never supported abortion, or had repented of being pro-abortion, just because he lived in a country that legalized abortion. Or, because he lived in a country that condoned legalized abortion in the past, or that no citizen could escape being considered pro-abortion until there were no people in America who personally supported abortion. That is the nonsensical and Christ-dishonoring approach proposed for racism according to social justice's critical race theory, which is antithetical to Scripture's teaching on sin, guilt, and forgiveness.

If the stain of racism exists until there is not a single racist, vestige of racism, indirect benefit of racism, or people liking certain things about people in the past while not condoning their racism or support of slavery, then the stain will continue to exist, and God's forgiveness and deliverance are powerless. Such a state of affairs would mean that the SBC and Southern Baptists need to continually repent with no hope of liberation, which is what it seems we have done and continue to do.

In 1995, at the SBC meeting in Atlanta, Georgia, the messengers passed a resolution on racial reconciliation. The first Whereas said, "Therefore, be it RESOLVED, That we, the messengers to the Sesquicentennial meeting of the Southern Baptist Convention, assembled in Atlanta, Georgia, June 20–22, 1995, unwaveringly denounce racism, in all its forms, as deplorable sin; and repenting of the racism that had been a part of the SBC." The fourth Whereas says, "Be it further RESOLVED, That we apologize to all African-Americans for condoning and/or perpetuating individual and systemic racism in our lifetime; and we genuinely repent of racism of which we have been guilty, whether consciously (Ps 19:13) or unconsciously (Lev 4:27)."[12] The resolution passed with a standing ovation. I was there and stood and cheered with everyone else.

Yet, in 2015, at the SBC meeting in Columbus, Ohio, President Ronnie Floyd led the messengers in an extended period devoted to racial reconciliation, which included the confession of sin, repentance, and prayer.

Then, in 2016, at the SBC convention meeting in St. Louis, Missouri, in a call for unity, a resolution was passed regarding the Confederate

12. "Resolution on Racial Reconciliation," paras. 1, 4.

flag. The third resolve stated, "That, we call our brothers and sisters in Christ to discontinue the display of the Confederate battle flag as a sign of solidarity of the whole Body of Christ, including our African American brothers and sisters."[13]

The very next year, in 2017, at the SBC convention meeting in Phoenix, Arizona, a resolution was passed against the Alt-right. The first three resolves are as follows. Be it "RESOLVED, That the messengers to the Southern Baptist Convention, meeting in Phoenix, Arizona, June 13–14, 2017, decry every form of racism, including alt-right white supremacy, as antithetical to the Gospel of Jesus Christ; and be it further RESOLVED, That we denounce and repudiate white supremacy and every form of racial and ethnic hatred as a scheme of the devil intended to bring suffering and division to our society; and be it further RESOLVED, That we acknowledge that we still must make progress in rooting out any remaining forms of intentional or unintentional racism in our midst."[14]

For more examples of the SBC repenting about its racism, see the book *Removing the Stain of Racism From the SBC.*[15] In December 2018, the SBTS publicly repented of its racist and white supremacist past, producing an over-seventy-page document.

In April 2018, in Louisville, Kentucky, David Platt (when he was president of the International Mission Board) and Ligon Duncan, while speaking at a Together for the Gospel event, confessed to the world they bear the stain of racism.[16]

Critical race theory racism permits no sufficient repentance, so the SBC and white people must continually repent of racism, even if a person in the SBC never had a racist thought. Continual repentance, according to critical race theory, is because its repentance is impotent, whereas repentance in Scripture is of God and, therefore, omnipotent. The ineffectiveness of repentance in critical race theory is antithetical to the gospel. Peter says, "The Lord is not slow about His promise, as some count slowness, but is patient toward you, not wishing for any to perish but for all to come to repentance" (2 Pet 3:9).

---

13. "On Sensitivity and Unity," para. 12.

14. "On the Anti-gospel," paras. 15–17.

15. For more resolutions on black and white relations in the SBC dating back to 1845, see *Removing the Stain of Racism from the Southern Baptist Convention, xxxv.*

16. Thenewcalvinist, "Stain," 51:36–49.

Some SBC pastors no longer go to the convention because they feel enough is enough. They ask, how many times do we have to repent as a convention? Biblically, a Christian can repent of racism and confess it (1 John 1:9) and be forgiven. But not so with critical race theory. The inability to effectively repent and be forgiven is why Dr. E. S. Williams says, "All cultural Marxism offers is a desolate form of eternal warfare between ever more narrowly defined groups of offended minorities."[17] So is repentance not sufficient to remove the stain? Apparently not.

Biblically, anyone through faith in Christ (John 3:16) and confession as a Christian (1 John 1:9) can be forgiven of racism. We can be forgiven because of the inexhaustible mercy of God (Ps 103:12; Heb 8:12). If our repentance is toward God, he remembers our sin no more, and we have no basis for speaking of our stain of racism or sin and guilt of racism as ongoing and in need of repentance and forgiveness. To do so is a denial of our forgiveness in Christ (John 3:16; 1 John 1:9). It is a denial of the very thing that makes the gospel, which means good news. Their zealousness about racism, as understood through the lens of critical race theory, intersectionality, and social justice, cannot be described as gospel-centered or promoting the gospel because they minimize the very point of the gospel. It is only critical race theory's ill-defined racism from which a white person cannot be freed.

Scripture's Omnipotent Forgiveness

Judgment Is Personal

- "But from the tree of the knowledge of good and evil you shall not eat, for in the day that you eat from it you will surely die" (Gen 2:17).

- "The person who sins will die. The son will not bear the punishment for the father's iniquity, nor will the father bear the punishment for the son's iniquity; the righteousness of the righteous will be upon himself, and the wickedness of the wicked will be upon himself. But if the wicked man turns from all his sins which he has committed and observes all My statutes and practices justice and righteousness, he shall surely live; he shall not die" (Ezek 18:20–21).

17. Thenewcalvinist, "Stain," 11:16–24.

- "The Lord has looked down from heaven upon the sons of men To see if there are any who understand, Who seek after God. They have all turned aside, together they have become corrupt; There is no one who does good, not even one" (Ps 14:1–3).

We are all in the same situation of being individually responsible for our sins.

God's Heart

- "For I have no pleasure in the death of anyone who dies," declares the Lord God. "Therefore, repent and live" (Ezek 18:32).
- "For the Son of Man did not come to destroy men's lives, but to save them" (Luke 9:56).
- "For the Son of Man has come to save that which was lost" (Matt 18:11).

Forgiveness Is for All

- But Jesus was saying, "Father, forgive them; for they do not know what they are doing" (Luke 23:34).
- And He said to him, "Truly I say to you, today you shall be with Me in Paradise" (Luke 23:43).
- "And that repentance for forgiveness of sins would be proclaimed in His name to all the nations, beginning from Jerusalem" (Luke 24:47).
- Peter said to them, "Repent, and each of you be baptized in the name of Jesus Christ for the forgiveness of your sins" (Acts 2:38).
- "Of Him all the prophets bear witness that through His name everyone who believes in Him receives forgiveness of sins" (Acts 10:43).
- "The Spirit and the bride say, 'Come.' And let the one who hears say, 'Come.' And let the one who is thirsty come; let the one who wishes take the water of life without cost" (Rev 22:17).
- "If we confess our sins, He is faithful and righteous to forgive us our sins and to cleanse us from all unrighteousness" (1 John 1:9).

A Corruption of Consequence

Once Saved, A Person Is Not What He Was

- "Therefore if anyone is in Christ, he is a new creature; the old things passed away; behold, new things have come" (2 Cor 5:17).

Only in cultural Marxism and critical race theory does the stain of racism continue beyond repentance because critical race theory considers someone a racist, white supremacist, because of the color of their skin or the group to which they belong. I do not doubt that those I have mentioned would affirm the truthfulness of all these Scriptures. Furthermore, I believe they strongly believe them. However, they either minimize the great truths of God's omnipotent forgiveness and work in the sinner's life or totally ignore them when dealing with the stain of racism; that is not reflective of Scripture but only critical race theory.

Contrary to critical race theory, having racist ancestors or growing up in a racist culture does not make a person a racist any more than someone having an ancestor who performed abortions or grows up in a culture that benefited from abortion tax dollars makes them pro-abortion. Nor does having ancestors who brewed white lightning or grew up in a culture that benefitted from profits from the sale of the alcohol or the jobs derived from the alcohol make a person a promoter of drunkenness.

I live in a culture saturated with alcohol and drunkards, but that does not make me pro-alcohol in any sense. I do not need to repent of any privileges I receive indirectly from alcohol sales (highways paid in part by alcohol taxes) because I oppose the sale of all alcohol. Remember, in contrast to the impotence of critical race theory's repentance, when a person repents and trusts Jesus Christ as Savior, he is forgiven, regenerated, and transformed (Isa 1:18; 1 Cor 6:11). Paul says, "Brethren, I do not regard myself as having laid hold of it yet; but one thing I do: forgetting what lies behind and reaching forward to what lies ahead, I press on toward the goal for the prize of the upward call of God in Christ Jesus" (Phil 3:13–14).

We can repent of having an abortion, providing an abortion, counseling for abortion, or supporting abortion and move on by repenting and walking in God's forgiveness and being pro-life. But with critical race theory's racism, white supremacy, we are imprisoned in that sin because we are white and belong to the majority. This being true, one must ask how such a system can provide neutral analytical tools?

9

Resolution 9

Critical Race Theory and Intersectionality as Analytical Tools

I BELIEVE THE ADOPTION of SBC Resolution 9 at the 2019 Southern Baptist Convention meeting in Birmingham, Alabama, was a watershed event. It did not signal trouble on the horizon, but rather it indicated to many there was already severe doctrinal trouble in some of our seminaries and entities. Dr. Curtis Woods chaired the Resolutions Committee at this meeting. He appears to be the, or at least a contributing architect of Resolution 9 that was passed at the convention. Before presenting that Resolution 9, the committee rejected the original Resolution that was written and submitted by Stephen Michael Feinstein, which was against using critical race theory/intersectionality for any purpose.[1]

Resolution 9 adopted critical race theory and intersectionality as "analytical tools." The second Whereas states, "Critical race theory is a set of analytical tools that explain how race has and continues to function in society, and intersectionality is the study of how different personal characteristics overlap and inform one's experience."[2]

The problem is that uncoupling "analytical tools" from the origin of such an ungodly philosophy so that the influence is absent is practically impossible. Think about Darwin, Freud, or higher criticism and cults who get

1. See Appendix 4.

2. "On Critical Race Theory And Intersectionality," para. 1. Also, see Appendix 2 and Appendix 3.

some things right. We do not need to use Darwin to analyze God's creation in Genesis, higher criticism (liberal theology) to analyze biblical theology and the Scriptures, Freud to analyze man, or porn to analyze sexuality.

While Dr. Mohler appears to grant a measure of approval to Resolution 9, he does clearly warn,

> It is true that both can be deployed as analytical tools. The problem is, as Christians understand, that analytical tools very rarely remain merely analytical tools.
>
> Ideas, as we know, do have consequences and one of the most lamentable consequences, but the main consequence of critical race theory and intersectionality is identity politics, and identity politics can only rightly be described as antithetical to the gospel of Jesus Christ. We have to see identity politics as disastrous to the culture and nothing less than devastating for the church of the Lord Jesus Christ.[3]

Had Dr. Mohler spoken so forthrightly while Resolution 9 was being considered, which he could have done, his comments would have been significant. But, his words mean much less in light of his silence before the adoption of the Resolution.

When the Resolutions Committee later tried to defend Resolution 9 against continued disapproval, which did nothing to solve the problem opponents like me have with it, Mohler swiftly tweeted, "I appreciate the BP & members of the 2019 Resolutions Committee talking here about Resolution 9. This the right tone. I am sure it is released in good faith."[4] Once again, Dr. Mohler quickly takes his stand with the woke.

It is the comparison of the adopted Resolution 9, which favors critical race theory and intersectionality, with the original by Stephen Michael Feinstein, which called for removing critical race theory and intersectionality from SBC institutions and churches, that underscores the favor that the Resolutions committee has for critical race theory and intersectionality.

The last two resolves of the original Resolution 9 written by Feinstein say:

> RESOLVED, That Southern Baptist institutions need to make progress in rooting out the intentional promulgation of critical race theory and intersectionality in both our churches and institutions; and be it further

3. Mohler, "Briefing," paras. 39–40.
4. Mohler, "Real Network of Southern Baptists."

RESOLVED, That we earnestly pray, both for those who advocate ideologies meant to divide believers along intersectional lines and those who are thereby deceived, that they may see their error through the light of the Gospel, repent of these anti-Gospel beliefs, and come to know the peace and love of Christ through redeemed fellowship in the Kingdom of God, which is established from every nation, tribe, people, and language.[5]

I suggest the following will take place unless the convention outright rejects critical race theory and intersectionality. The use of critical race theory and intersectionality as analytical tools will at first sully and distract from biblical teaching. Then it will subtly deemphasize Scripture at vital points while emphasizing critical race theory ideas. Then biblical terms will be replaced with critical race theory defined terms, which will ultimately lead to a significant and costly corruption of the biblical message.[6] It cannot help but undermine the gospel because it is materialistic Marxism at its foundation, and it divides people (including Christians) into identities drawn from experience that separate people. It further provides people with more excuses to blame others for their plight. It also marginalizes the very essence of the good news gospel of immediate and complete forgiveness when anyone repents of any sin. All of which are antithetical to the spiritual truth of Scripture. Analytical tools do not exist in a sterile, non-ideological vacuum. They lead to conclusions. I have yet to see how the use of Marxist tools can lead to a better understanding of the culture, people, or Scripture (interpretation or application) than using theology drawn from Scripture.[7]

The Bible is sufficient to analyze human relationships. It is a book about relationships in time and eternity. These relationships include multifaceted relationships within the creation and with creation's Creator. Reliance on the sufficiency of Scripture is not meant to mean that all knowledge about relationships exists only in the Scripture. It is to say that all essential knowledge about them does. And knowledge drawn from human experience

5. Feinstein, "SBC19 Resolution #9," paras. 39–40. See the full Resolution by Feinstein in Appendix 4.

6. For an example of this, one only needs to look at how pastoral counseling's adoption of secular psychology transformed it from biblically-based soul care to subjecting Scripture to science.

7. Even if it can be demonstrated that some insight might be gained by the use of these tools, such fails to show that the same cannot be gleaned by safer and more biblical tools. Moreover, it does not demonstrate how such tools can be safely used on a broad scale; inevitably, this will lead to corruption.

must reflect the Scripture's teaching on relationships, God, human beings, and God's great redemptive plan, which neither critical race theory nor intersectionality does.

10

What Racism Is Not and
What Christianity Can Do

Racism Is Not:

1. An all-white majority or church does not reflect racism any more than an all-black church does. Racism is a matter of the heart and not the color of one's skin.

2. A racist statement does not make a racist any more than a dumb statement makes someone stupid, or a brilliant statement makes someone brilliant.

3. Living in a racist culture or having the same skin color as a racist or even many racists does not make someone a racist. Benefiting from a culture with racism does not necessarily make someone a racist. For example, our society has significant crime, and we benefit by the creation of security companies and security devices (jobs, taxes paid) as well as additional police and hospital jobs, but that does not make us criminals or pro-criminal. Genuine racism, not critical race theory's imitation racism, flows from the heart (Matt 15:18–19) as does all sin and cannot be determined by a person's skin pigmentation. Most importantly, it can be washed away by faith in Jesus Christ (John 1:29; 3:16) and confessed and forgiven if committed after a person is saved (1 John 1:9).

What Christianity Can Do:

1. Christianity unites humanity in that all are created in God's image and salvationally loved by him. As salvation in Christ broke down the barriers between Jew and gentile, it breaks down all other barriers (Eph 2:14–15). Salvation in Christ makes all, regardless of skin color or past sins, one body with one God and one fellowship (Eph 4:4–6).

2. There is no actual racial divide in the true church, for we are all one in Christ (Eph 4:4–7). I am judged by God for what I have done and not for what my ancestors did (Ezek 18:20–22). If, in the past, a person was a racist in his heart (as with lust, anger, or any other sin), he can be completely forgiven through Christ (1 John 1:9). Voddie Baucham rightly declares that true racial reconciliation is not something we have to achieve, instead "It's something you and I have to believe because Christ has already achieved it. It is done; it is real. We are one in Christ."[1] We may need to be reminded and walk in the fullness of what Christ achieved in the same way we walk in fellowship with God (1 John 1:3).

   Commenting on Ephesians 2, Baucham says, "There are different cultural distinctions among us and other things that distinguish us: our languages and things of this nature. But that's different than saying we have real legitimate things that separate us. Why is this important? Because if the things that we believe separate us are made up, and we see in this text that a real separation that God created is overcome by the blood of Christ, if the blood of Jesus can obliterate a real distinction that God himself created, then how much more can it get rid of artificial distinctions that fallen men created?"[2]

3. We do not need critical race theory and intersectionality to understand our divisions or be reconciled with others. We need Christ, and we need to walk in the fullness of the presence of the one who reconciled us so that we do not look on such superficial distinctions as skin pigmentation. We are ambassadors of reconciliation to God and man through Christ (2 Cor 5:14–21). Paul declares that the Jews and gentiles, who were as divided as any two groups could be, are united and become one in salvation.

1. Founders Ministries, "Racial Reconciliation," 45:31–47.
2. Baucham, "Irreconcilable Views," 54:03.

Paul says, "Remember that you were at that time separate from Christ, excluded from the commonwealth of Israel, and strangers to the covenants of promise, having no hope and without God in the world. But now in Christ Jesus you who formerly were far off have been brought near by the blood of Christ. For He Himself is our peace, who made both groups into one and broke down the barrier of the dividing wall, by abolishing in His flesh the enmity, which is the Law of commandments contained in ordinances, so that in Himself He might make the two into one new man, thus establishing peace, and might reconcile them both in one body to God through the cross, by it having put to death the enmity" (Eph 2:12–16).

A friend of mine ministers to inmates in state prison, and he recently shared the following story about one of the inmates with whom he is working. Previously, the man was in prison, and while there, he belonged to a white supremacist gang. Later he was released from prison but then committed another crime. This time he was sent to the prison where my friend ministers.

In the fall of 2019, my friend led the inmate to Christ and has been discipling him ever since. Soon after he was saved, the white supremacist gang at this prison saw his white supremacist tattoo from his former life as a white supremacist. They told him they needed his help to beat up a black inmate. He refused to help and told them he is now a follower of Jesus Christ. The white supremacists beat him so severely that he spent over a month in the hospital. But he did not compromise, and he is still being discipled and following Christ.

Although he still bears the tattooed physical markings of being a white supremacist, he is not a white supremacist because he has become a new creation with a new heart, and his sins have been washed away (John 3:3; 2 Cor 5:17).

Isaiah said, "Come now, and let us reason together," says the Lord, "Though your sins are as scarlet, They will be as white as snow; Though they are red like crimson, They will be like wool" (Isa 1:18). The gospel is the great reconciler.

11

The Gospel Does Not Include Justice

THERE HAVE ALWAYS BEEN people who seek to add to the saving gospel of Jesus Christ. But any addition to the requirements of the gospel, as presented in the New Testament, is a corruption of the gospel, a corruption of consequence.

What is meant by the gospel? The word "gospel" simply means good news. In the New Testament, it is the good news of God providing salvation by faith in Jesus Christ. The gospel includes the message of the incarnate Jesus Christ dying on the cross as a substitutionary atonement for the sins of humanity (John 1:29; Heb 2:9) so that anyone can be saved by believing in him (John 3:16; Rom 10:9–10). God's acceptance of Christ's payment for the sins of humanity was made evident in that God raised him from the dead (Rom 4:25). Therefore, God is just to justify the ungodly who trust Christ (Rom 3:26; 4:5).

Paul succinctly describes the gospel as preached to the Corinthians, and their faith in the gospel resulted in their salvation. He says,

> Now I make known to you, brethren, the gospel which I preached to you, which also you received, in which also you stand, by which also you are saved, if you hold fast the word which I preached to you, unless you believed in vain. For I delivered to you as of first importance what I also received, that Christ died for our sins according to the Scriptures, and that He was buried, and that He was raised on the third day according to the Scriptures. (1 Cor 15:1–4)

Practically, the gospel answers the question of what must we share for a person to be saved from their sins and to be declared justified by God. It simply answers the question of the lost person, as seen in the encounter with the Philippian jailer. "And after he brought them out, he said, 'Sirs, what must I do to be saved?' They said, 'Believe in the Lord Jesus, and you will be saved, you and your household'" (Acts 16:30–31).

The Galatians had accepted the addition of keeping some of the Old Testament law as a requirement of the gospel. Paul rebuked the Galatians, saying,

> I am amazed that you are so quickly deserting Him who called you by the grace of Christ, for a different gospel; which is really not another; only there are some who are disturbing you and want to distort the gospel of Christ. But even if we, or an angel from heaven, should preach to you a gospel contrary to what we have preached to you, he is to be accursed! As we have said before, so I say again now, if any man is preaching to you a gospel contrary to what you received, he is to be accursed. (Gal 1:6–9)

The threat to the Galatians came from the Judaizers. These were Jewish Christians who believed that a person must exercise faith and keep Jewish religious customs like dietary laws and circumcision as taught in the Old Testament to be saved (Acts 15:1) and live the full Christian life. Faith in the gospel, which is relying solely on Christ's death, burial, and resurrection as atonement for sin, was not enough. They also sought to impose these additions on the gospel to the gentiles. Their modification of the biblical gospel created a different gospel, which was not really another gospel but a corruption of the gospel (Gal 1:6–7).

Paul's confrontation with Peter's compromise with the Judaizers concisely describes the problems. Paul said,

> But when I saw that they were not straightforward about the truth of the gospel, I said to Cephas in the presence of all, "If you, being a Jew, live like the Gentiles and not like the Jews, how is it that you compel the Gentiles to live like Jews? We are Jews by nature and not sinners from among the Gentiles; nevertheless knowing that a man is not justified by the works of the Law but through faith in Christ Jesus, even we have believed in Christ Jesus, so that we may be justified by faith in Christ and not by the works of the Law; since by the works of the Law no flesh will be justified." (Gal 2:14–16)

Peter was a Jew by birth, but after he was saved by faith in Christ, he lived like a gentile; that is, without trusting the Old Testament law. Later, because he feared the Judaizers, Peter compromised the gospel by accepting the Jews' mix of law and grace and then joining them in requiring that the gentiles keep the law as a necessary part of salvation. The verb form of "Judaize," *Ioudiazo*, appears in Galatians 2:14. It is translated "to live like Jews." Judaizers mixed the law and faith as a requirement for salvation and living the Christian life after being saved. They sought to impose the same on gentiles, which is a corruption of the gospel at its core. As Paul says, "Knowing that a man is not justified by the works of the Law but through faith in Christ Jesus . . . since by the works of the Law no flesh will be justified" (Gal 2:16). See also Romans 3:28, 30.

Some emphasize that the gospel was corrupted when the Judaizers demanded the gentiles exercise faith and keep the law ("live like Jews," Gal 2:14), but that is inaccurate; it was also a corruption for the Jews. To add keeping the law or anything to salvation by faith (Eph 2:8) is a corruption of the gospel for anyone, including the Jew. Paul said, "Since indeed God who will justify the circumcised by faith and the uncircumcised through faith is one" (Rom 3:30).

Social justice is composed of some of the critical components of cultural Marxism and insists that all groups should have equal access to all privileges, wealth, opportunity, and equal outcomes regardless of other circumstances such as individual merit or contributions. Justice is accomplished by favoring one group (the oppressed/minority/righteous) and punishing another group (the oppressors/majority/sinners) by the redistribution of wealth, power, and privilege.[1] Therefore, social justice means justice will be accomplished when there are equal outcomes. For true equality, there must be a redistribution of wealth and power to the oppressed. Social justice contains many aspects such as racial reconciliation, economic equality, prison reform, and the plight of the homeless, all of which arise from whatever a minority group deems to be an injustice inflicted by the majority upon the minority. The solution is defined by the social justice advocates rather than Scripture, which sees some of the same

---

1. Cultural Marxism proposes a clash between the oppressed (minorities) and the oppressor (majority). The "majority groups are typically defined as privileged and oppressive, with minority groups accordingly labeled underprivileged and oppressed." Thenewcalvinist, "Stain," 9:36–44. In the USA and most of Europe, this means that white people are the oppressors, white supremacists, and the oppressed are the blacks but other minorities are also included.

problems but often defines them and their treatment strikingly different from that of social justice warriors.

Thomas Sowell reminds us of two crucial facts; each points out why socialism never works. One is that when we speak of wealth, we should think of the human mind because that is the source of wealth. You can take wealth (material wealth) away from people and give it to others, but the people who created that wealth are the real *source* of wealth; material wealth alone does not create wealth. Physical wealth can be stolen, redistributed, and depleted, but human capital (the mind), which is the source of wealth, is inseparable from the person. Thus, the welfare state and socialism stop the development of human capital, which ultimately leads to poverty.[2] The Soviet Union, China, Cuba, Cambodia, Vietnam, and Venezuela come to mind.

The second is that while it is possible to offer equality of opportunity, it is impossible to provide equality of the probability of success.[3] Yet, that is what social justice, socialism, Black Liberation Theology, and Marxism promise and demand.[4] And that is why they are always doomed to fail to achieve what is promised; even worse, they lead to greater poverty and suffering. Well-meaning evangelicals have been drawn into believing in socialistic justice as they are naively facilitating the cause by their wokeness and adopting phrases like Black Lives Matter.[5]

Democratic Socialists of America like to claim Norway, Sweden, and Denmark as examples of socialist success stories, but there are several problems with the legitimacy of that claim. For example, writing for the Heritage Foundation, Anthony B. Kim states:

---

2. We should not confuse the wealth of the leaders in socialistic states with what happens to the people, which is poverty. See Hoover Institution, "Wealth, Poverty, and Politics." See also Hoover Institution, "Thomas Sowell Is Back Again."

3. Equality of opportunity does not mean every human can get the exact same opportunity because that is impossible in a time and space continuum. It does mean that each person who gets the same opportunity as someone else should be treated equally. For example, if a black person and a white person apply for a job, each should be treated equally and evaluated on their abilities, not their skin color.

4. Hoover Institution, "Thomas Sowell Talks about His New Book."

5. The rejection of Black Lives Matter as an organization or slogan is not equivalent to saying the lives of black people do not matter. Instead, it is a rejection of the BLM organization, the use of its Marxian mantra, and their quest to destroy capitalism, America, and, if it were possible, Christianity. I believe Christians should speak biblically by proclaiming that all people are created in the image of God, and, therefore, all people matter.

A Corruption of Consequence

By the YDSA's [Young Democratic Socialists of America] definition, socialism entails a centrally planned economy with nation-
alized means of production. Although these countries have high
income taxes and provide generous social programs, they remain
prosperous because of their free-market economies. Denmark
ranks as the 8th most economically free country in The Heritage
Foundation's Index of Economic Freedom, which cites free-market
policies and regulatory efficiency as reasons for the high standard
of living. Sweden is ranked 22nd and Norway 28th, both with
similar descriptions of thriving private sectors and open markets.[6]
These three countries are clearly not operating under centrally
planned economies, or their economic freedom scores would be
significantly lower.[7]

Some evangelicals referred to as woke (seeing justice through the eyes
of the oppressed) or social justice warriors seek to make justice, which is
really socialistic justice, a definitional part of the gospel. That is, the complete gospel that is preached must include the requisite justice; accordingly,
they will speak of the gospel without social justice as an incomplete gospel.
(See chapter 13 for my response to Dr. Jarvis Williams's requiring racial
reconciliation as a "demand" of the gospel.)

Doing justice, or one's opinion about justice, is not a part of the gospel
we preach unto salvation. Seeking to make it a part of the gospel is a corruption of the gospel, similar to the way the Judaizers corrupted the gospel
by requiring the keeping of God's law. The point of the gospel, salvation, is
that before we are saved, we have not and cannot practice true justice (Rom
3:10–12), of which social justice is just another human sinful corruption.
God's impartial holy justice emanates from his being (1 Pet 1:16). Salvation, according to God's grace, mercy, and justice for every lost person, was
secured by Jesus Christ (1 John 2:2). It flows through the gospel and is given
to every person who trusts Christ as Savior. That is the gospel (Matt 18:11;
1 Cor 15:1–4; John 3:16; Titus 2:11).

The ones who believe are born again and forgiven (John 3:1–7; 2 Cor
5:17). All who become God's people through faith in the gospel are to live
lives in which God's justice and righteousness flow through us in all things
to all people (Lev 19:15; Amos 5:24; 2 Cor 5:14–20; 1 Pet 1:15). Therefore,
social justice is not biblical justice, and true righteousness and justice are
the results of the gospel, not a part of it definitionally or what it demands.

6. There are 195 countries in the world.
7. Kim and Howe, *Democratic Socialists*, 3.

For example, consider the issue of racism in social justice. Racism is a component of the injustices included in social justice. Social justice is a part of cultural Marxism, as is critical race theory. According to critical race theory, the concept of race was constructed by white people. Race serves as a mechanism for white people to oppress black people and promote pervasive institutional racism to maintain white supremacy. Cultural Marxism is composed of a broad set of ideas that serve as instruments for a societal transformation to bring about the redistribution of power and wealth.[8] White people need to repent of white supremacy and privilege (the majority), but black people (the minority) do not need to repent. Even if a white person has never had a genuinely racist thought or has repented of past (actual) racism, he is still a racist because he is of the white majority, and, therefore, his whiteness makes him a racist.[9]

Social justice and critical race theory are antithetical to the gospel and true justice. Social justice is based on man's sinful wisdom (determined by various minority groups), whereas biblical justice is based on God's holy character (1 Pet 1:16). Critical race theory's forgiveness through confession and repentance cannot effectively and completely change a person from being a racist. He will always be a racist because of his skin color or because he belongs to the majority, whereas biblical forgiveness makes a person forgiven, forever, and a new person (Rom 8:1; 2 Cor 5:17).

Critical race theory's guilt of racism or having suffered from racism is determined by whether the group the person belongs to is considered racist or is considered to have suffered from racism, even if the person as an individual never had a racist thought or suffered from racism. In contrast, biblical guilt or innocence is based on whether the individual personally acted like a racist or personally suffered from racism. Biblical racism occurs when a person views or treats a person of another ethnicity or race as inherently inferior. It is a sin because every person is created in the image of God (Gen 1:26–28).

Social justice and critical race theory say a person is responsible for other people's sins because of his skin pigmentation or because he belongs to the majority, whereas biblical racism says it is a matter of an individual's heart and actions, as is all sin (Matt 5:27–28; 15:19). Social justice and

8. Cultural Marxism is the application of Marxist concepts to marginalized groups rather than classes as in classical Marxism. For further definition of critical race theory, see Curry, "Critical Race Theory."

9. True racism is the belief that one's own race is inherently superior to another, and others, being inherently inferior, cannot overcome their inferiority.

critical race theory are materialistic perspectives, which mean that justice and injustice are determined by humans (social justice advocates) and, therefore, justice must be accomplished in this world. In contrast, biblical justice is spiritual, determined by God, and will not be fully realized until eternity. However, Christians should seek to make this world better by living righteous and merciful lives.

Therefore, social justice is not a part of the gospel but can only corrupt the gospel. The following lists will compare and contrast the faith teaching of Judaizers, social justice advocates, and the Bible.

The Judaizers Declare:

- The gospel requires faith in Christ and living like a Jew who keeps the law.
- Faith and keeping the law equal salvation.
- Grace and the law equal the gospel.
- Grace, faith, and doing justice, according to the law, is the gospel that results in salvation.

Social Justice Advocates Declare:

- The gospel requires faith in Christ and pursuing social justice.
- Faith and pursuing justice equal salvation.
- Grace and justice equal the gospel.
- Grace, faith, and doing justice, according to social justice, is the gospel that results in salvation.

The Bible Declares:

- The gospel requires faith in Christ (1 Cor 15:1–4).
- Faith in Christ equals salvation (John 3:18).
- Grace, through faith, equals salvation (Eph 2:8).

- Grace through faith in Christ dying for your sin, and nothing else, is the gospel that results in salvation (John 3:16).

Therefore, anyone who attaches social justice or any aspect of social justice, which is often abbreviated to justice, corrupts the gospel of Jesus Christ.

Biblical Justice Triumphs over Social Justice

Social Justice

WHILE SOCIAL JUSTICE AND cultural Marxism are not synonymous, they can rightly be used interchangeably as I have done.[1] They both seek forced redistribution of wealth and power from the groups who have it to the ones who do not. That is to say, from the majority to the minority, and in America, that first and foremost means from the white people to the black people. This transfer of wealth and power is regardless of personal merit or how hard a person had to work for his wealth. The majority must be punished to bring about social justice, and the minority must be rewarded by receiving the power and wealth of the majority. Personal merit is not a factor; only group identity determines whether one should be rewarded or punished. A person is guilty for someone else's sin even if he does not agree with those who committed the sin or even if the actual person who committed the sin lived hundreds of years ago. What determines guilt is based on if you belong to the guilty group. Reparations, in the name of social justice, lead to the absurd place of people who disapprove of slavery and have never owned slaves giving money to people who have never been slaves because some people whom we do not know owned slaves or were slaves. Furthermore, most Southerners did not own slaves.

---

1. "In the 1950's, [Herbert] Marcuse stated the Marxist revolution would not be brought about by 'the proletariat' but by a coalition of blacks, feminist women, homosexuals, and students. This is where the term 'Cultural Marxism' comes from, as it is applied to marginalized groups rather than class." Kirschner, "Cultural Marxism," para. 29.

Daina Ramey Berry, Associate Professor of History and African and African Diaspora Studies, the University of Texas at Austin, says, "Roughly 25 percent of all Southerners owned slaves."[2] In contrast to the popular narrative that claims the first blacks on American soil were slaves, Berry also notes, "Africans first arrived in America in the late 16th century not as slaves but as explorers together with Spanish and Portuguese explorers."[3] In anticipation of potential fallacious white privilege charges, I think it is worth noting that Professor Berry is a black person (as is Thomas Sowell, Shelby Steele, Walter Williams, and Robert L. Woodson, whom I quote throughout this book). This percentage of slave owners is in stark contrast to the popular description or inference that promotes the idea that the vast majority of whites or even all whites owned slaves. Are we to seek reparations from people whose ancestors did not own slaves? Is that justice? Sowell tells us, "There were thousands of other blacks in the antebellum South who were commercial slaveowners, just like their white counterparts."[4]

Additionally, "An estimated one-third of the 'free persons of color' in New Orleans were slaveowners and thousands of these slaveowners volunteered to fight for the Confederacy during the Civil War."[5] Sowell further states, "Black slaveowners were even more common in the Caribbean."[6] As you might well imagine, these blacks supported the institution of slavery.[7] Should we seek reparations from these black slaveowners for the descendants of their slaves? Add to this that many whites fought to free slaves utilizing the underground railroad and other measures before the Civil War; many whites supported the emancipation of slaves and died for their freedom. Furthermore, what shall we do about other mistreated groups in America's past, such as the Jews and even many whites by the Britons?

---

2. Of course, the percentage nationally would be significantly less. Berry, "American Slavery," para. 13.

3. Berry, "American Slavery," para. 11.

4. Sowell, *Black Rednecks*, 127. See also Gray, *History of Agriculture*, 528; Koger, *Black Slaveowners*; Rankin, "Impact of the Civil War," 380, 385; Gatewood, *Aristocrats of Color*, 83; Berlin, *Slaves without Masters*, 124, 386; Genovese, "Slave States of North America," 270; Morgan, "Black Life in Eighteenth-Century Charleston," 212; and Powers, *Black Charlestonians*, 48–50, 72.

5. Sowell, *Black Rednecks*, 127. See also Gatewood, *Aristocrats of Color*, 83; Berlin, *Slaves without Masters*, 124, 386; and Rankin, "Impact of the Civil War," 380, 385.

6. Sowell, *Black Rednecks*, 127. See Handler and Sio, "Barbados," 245–46, and Elisabeth, "French Antilles," 165–66.

7. Sowell, *Black Rednecks*, 127.

A Corruption of Consequence

Then there was the enslavement of white Europeans by the Barbary pirates. Jeff Grabmeier notes that Robert Davis, professor of history at Ohio State University, "has calculated that between 1 million and 1.25 million European Christians were captured and forced to work in North Africa from the 16th to 18th centuries."[8] Regarding white enslavement, Sowell remarks, "European slaves were still being sold on the auction block in Egypt, years after the Emancipation Proclamation freed blacks in the United States."[9] Thus, whites were fighting to end slavery in America and England, while white Europeans were still being enslaved in Egypt.

In comparison between the number of slaves in the United States and even the entire Western Hemisphere and elsewhere, Sowell notes, "Even larger number[s] of Africans [were] enslaved in the Islamic countries . . . and North Africa."[10] Yet, we hear little or nothing from blacks who hate whites hating Muslims. Instead, social justice makes Muslims an oppressed group at the hands of Christians. Slavery has existed all over the world for thousands of years. This is not to minimize the barbarism of slavery in the United States; instead, it is to give context to slavery discussions in America so that people do not think slavery is the racist product of America, which transforms slavery into a weaponized utility for racial aggression against whites.

Given the practice of slavery around the world for millennia, and that most enslavement was of people of the same race, Sowell concludes, "In short, racism was neither necessary nor sufficient for slavery, whose origins antedated racism by centuries. Racism was a result, not a cause, of slavery."[11] Regarding the European slave trade of Africans, Sowell comments, "Far from being targeted by Europeans for racial reasons . . . Africa was resorted to . . . only after centuries of Europeans enslaving other Europeans had been brought to an end."[12] The fact is that "slavery was . . . an established institution in the Western Hemisphere before Columbus' ships ever appeared on the horizon."[13] And even during the time of the African

8. Grabmeier. "When Europeans Were Slaves," para. 3. See also Sowell, *Black Rednecks*, 112.

9. Sowell, *Black Rednecks*, 112.

10. Sowell, *Black Rednecks*, 112.

11. Sowell, *Black Rednecks*, 128.

12. Sowell, *Black Rednecks*, 115.

13. Sowell, *Black Rednecks*, 112.

slave trade, "existing slaves continued to include peoples of many races living in many places around the world."[14]

Shall all races or groups seek reparations from those who enslaved or treated them as subhuman? If this form of *justice* prevails, the madness will not and cannot stop. Moreover, before blacks promote reparations against white America, they would do well to probe the history of slavery a little deeper. The African slaves that were brought to the West from Africa were caught and enslaved by black Africans first. At the time of the African slave trade with the West, "Africa was largely ruled by Africans, who established the conditions under which slave sales took place."[15] By the time Europeans established empires there, the "Atlantic slave trade had already ended."[16] The Africans sold some of those they enslaved to the West. But at the height of the slave trade to the West, the Africans kept more slaves than they traded to the West. The fact is that the Africans practiced slavery before, during, and after they provided slaves to Westerners.[17]

The bestselling book and mini-series, *Roots*, by Alex Haley, portrayed white men invading and conquering Africa to capture Africans for Western slavery, but that is a myth, a very damaging myth. When Haley was challenged about the historical accuracy of *Roots*, he said, "I tried to give my people a myth to live by."[18] The truth is, "The region of West Africa from which Kunte Kinte supposedly came was one of the great slave-trading regions of the continent—before, during, and after the white man arrived."[19] Additionally, when I refer to black people, I do not mean all black people are proponents of socialistic justice because many are not.[20]

Although Great Britain and America are guilty of the sin of slavery, and I would say particularly those who claim the name of Christ, the end of slavery around the world came about by Christians and Great Britain. Sowell says, "Europeans . . . became . . . the destroyers of slavery around the world."[21] Only the West developed a moral conscience against slavery.

---

14. Sowell, *Black Rednecks*, 115.

15. Sowell, *Black Rednecks*, 121.

16. Sowell, *Black Rednecks*, 121.

17. Sowell, *Black Rednecks*, 120.

18. Nobile, "Uncovering Roots," 34.

19. Sowell, *Black Rednecks*, 120.

20. Some black scholars who argue against such things: Thomas Sowell, Walter Williams, Shelby Steele, and Robert L. Woodson Sr.

21. Sowell, *Black Rednecks*, 116.

"Within Western civilization, the principal impetus for the abolition of slavery came first from very conservative religious activists—people who would today be called 'the religious right.' Clearly, this story is not 'politically correct' in today's terms. Hence it is ignored as if it never happened."[22]

Measures such as graduated tax systems, reparations paid by those who did not sin for what previous generations did, and affirmative action may be implemented in the move toward socialistic justice, but such enactments are almost certain to fail to bring in a just socialistic Utopia. Such will almost certainly require a Marxian revolution to overthrow capitalism and Christianity. By overthrowing Christianity, I do not mean that Marxism or any other satanic or earthly power can conquer or destroy Christianity because they cannot (Matt 16:18). Instead, I mean Marxism will seek to eliminate any influence or public presence of Christianity and Christian principles. To overthrow capitalism and America will most likely require the use of anarchical riots in which there is massive destruction of private property, killing of innocent people, and forceful intimidation of government, law enforcement, and law-abiding citizens. We have observed this in the incalculably destructive riots across America in the wake of the death of George Floyd, which has, directly and indirectly, resulted in the deaths of many innocent people. It has unleashed inestimable destruction of private property and livelihood, as well as the intimidation of governments resulting in defunding police departments.[23]

The average onlooker who thinks the protests and riots are only about outrage over the death of Floyd or racial injustice is perplexed by the black rioters killing innocent black people, including children, and the destruction of their livelihood and property.[24] They are baffled why there is not an outcry by the protestors over the black innocents being killed by the rioters, black on black killings that number more than all the people ever enslaved in America,[25] and by the nearly one-thousand black babies killed by

22. Sowell, *Black Rednecks*, 116.

23. Noman, Oklahoma, where I live, did vote on June 15, 2020, to decrease funding for our police department by $885,000.00. This seems to have been done because of the city council's liberal bias, and to a significant degree, because of the protests in Norman and threats of rioters across the country in fulfillment of the BLM agenda to nationally defund police departments. Felder, "Norman Council Reduced Police Budget," and Black Lives Matter, "#DefundThePolice."

24. Rojas, "It's Got to Stop."

25. Levin, "Bob Woodson Joins Mark Levin."

abortion every day in America.[26] And rightly so because it is not just about having equal opportunity or equal treatment for everyone under the law for the cultural Marxists. It is about equal outcomes for everyone, regardless of personal merit. To the Marxist, unequal outcome alone is the irrefutable evidence of injustice. To reach their Utopic state of equal outcome will require the overthrow of capitalism, America, and with that, Christianity.

Many Christians race to identify with marches led by Black Lives Matter (BLM) and to shout and carry signs saying BLM. To suggest Christians should say all people matter because all people are created in the image of God (Gen 1:26–27) can result in personal attacks by Christians who embrace the BLM mantra and BLM-led marches. At a minimum, they will argue with you in defense of using BLM language over biblical wording. My conversations have led me to conclude that it does not matter to some if you show them the ungodly beliefs and agendas of BLM: "We foster a queer-affirming network. When we gather, we do so with the intention of freeing ourselves from the tight grip of heteronormative thinking, or rather, the belief that all in the world are heterosexual (unless s/he or they disclose otherwise) [and] *We disrupt the Western-prescribed nuclear family structure requirement*"[27] (italics added). The very thing both black and white people need to thrive is to grow up in a nuclear (biblical) family, which is one of BLM's targets for destruction. This is not surprising given that two of the founders are lesbians. For whatever reason, these Christians are committed to the BLM group mantra. While they may disavow the other unbiblical agendas listed on the BLM website as illustrated here, they will not disavow the BLM saying. They will often don a BLM t-shirt instead of one proclaiming Christ as the answer.

As previously mentioned, two of the BLM founders and leaders claim to be trained Marxists. Patrisse Cullors says, "We actually do have an ideological frame. Myself, and Alicia Garza, in particular, are trained organizers; we are trained Marxists. We are super versed in ideological theories. What we really try to do is build a movement that can be used by many,

26. "Genocide: Black Abortions in America."

27. As of September 22, 2020, BLM has removed their page, "What We Believe," from its website, which included this information. They have not disowned these founding ideals, but only removed them to obscure who they really are. I suspect they began to realize that such honesty was not as widely accepted as if they simply portrayed themselves as defending blacks unjustly killed by the police out of racism. I have retained their original words so that people can know who they really are and what they desire to do. See the bibliography for a link to an archive page where you can still read their words.

many black folks."[28] Even when some of the woke, BLM mantra advocates learn this, they continue seeking to justify saying BLM, which advertises the BLM brand rather than fleeing to the clear declarations of Scripture.

As is true in Marxism, social justice emphasizes group identity rather than individual identity. The division is between the majority groups who are the oppressors, and the minority groups who are the oppressed. In critical theory, of which social justice is a part, this division serves as the necessary structure for the transformation of society.[29] The group identity of the oppressed may be comprised of people who did not directly suffer the wrongs. It may also be made up of biblically sinful groups such as homosexuals and non-cisgenders.[30] Sometimes non-cisgenders are referred to with terms like transgender or gender fluidity. Cultural Marxism is the progenitor of identity politics.

The group identity of the oppressors may be composed of people who did not personally contribute to the wrongs against the oppressed group, either in their hearts or by their actions. They are deemed oppressors merely because of their skin color or majority status. For example, they may not be guilty of genuine racism, which is the belief that one's race is inherently superior, and other races are inherently inferior and, therefore, cannot overcome their inferiority. Or the person may have repented of believing in genuine racism. But, if the person is white and a part of the majority, he is still a racist according to social justice and critical race theory because he is white and a part of the majority.[31] He is a racist because critical race theory says that race is a social construct of white people designed to maintain their place of supremacy and privilege. Even if a person has truly repented of racism, does not consciously hold to any racist's thoughts, and does not act racist, he is still said to be implicitly racist. To wit, every white person is forever unconsciously racist because that is what whiteness entails; hence,

28. The Real News Network, "Short History of Black Lives Matter," 7:10. See also John, "Black Lives Matter Co-Founder Confirms."

29. Critical theory, of which critical race theory is a part, is a Marxian-inspired socialistic philosophy emanating from the Frankfurt school. Unlike other social theories, which seek to explain society, critical theory seeks to change society. It also includes the presumption of an oppression/oppressed dynamic. The theory draws significantly on the thought of Karl Marx, Friedrich Engels, and Sigmund Freud.

30. A non-cisgender is one whose chosen gender identity does not correspond to one's biological sex at birth.

31. Critical race theory espouses that race is created by the white population in order to keep the black population in a subservient role to advance the interests of the white population. Race is not related to biology.

there is no resolve, deliverance, or rescue from the sin of racism, even from Christ himself. Their rendering is "Behold, the Lamb of God who takes away the sin of the world"—except for racism, which is blasphemous.

Equal opportunity and being treated equally before the laws of man are not sufficient. Nor is standing equally before the law of God sufficient. Social justice is based on group identity that minimizes or ignores individual merit for benefits sought or guilt for wrongs punished. In social justice, as in critical race theory, merit or guilt is based upon such things as skin color, sex, illegal immigrant status, or sexual preference because they determine whether that group is a majority or minority, and therefore the oppressor or oppressed. Social justice is composed of various dissimilar groups of oppressors and oppressed (whites and blacks, heterosexuals and homosexuals, Christians and non-Christians), and, accordingly, intentionally disunifies society.

For example, notice how often the progressives (liberals) depict conservative Christians (the majority) in a negative light and Muslims (the minority) in a positive light even though Islam tortures and murders innocent people in the name of Allah every day. Moreover, if America were to become an Islamic state, the same liberals who sympathized and promoted Islam would be summarily stripped of the freedom to espouse their progressive views or even executed for their opinions. Their romantic love of ideals like equal outcomes, no poverty, and their disdain for America and capitalism (which by the way, allowed them to live better than any people in history) will usher them into the harsh reality of an Islamic state that will silence them and their dreams. Social justice advocates are the determiners of who are the oppressors (sinners) and who are the oppressed (non-sinners) and what the oppressors will have to do to achieve forgiveness (which is never competed) for themselves and equity for the oppressed.

Biblical Justice

This type of justice emanates from God's holy and loving nature (Lev 19:2; 1 Pet 1:15; 1 John 4:8) and is impartial (Acts 10:34; Jas 2:9). He communicates his standard of justice through his holy Word (Jer 9:24; John 17:17). Everyone is created in the image of God and belongs to the human race (Gen 1:26–28). They are, therefore, equal in essence and under the same righteous standard of justice. Because everyone has personally sinned against God, everyone has fallen short of his holy justice (Rom 3:9–11).

A Corruption of Consequence

Each person is accountable for only his sin rather than the sins of his ancestors or any group to which he belongs unless he condones or participates in
the sin of the group (Ezek 18:19–21).

Because God is love (1 John 4:8, 16), he desires to save every person
from their due judgment for their sin, and he has provisioned so that everyone can be saved (Ezek 18:32; 33:11; John 1:29; 3:16; 20:30–31). Everyone
is saved from the just penalty for their sins in the same way, which is by repentance and faith in Christ for sins they actually committed against God's
holiness, whether in thought or deed (Matt 5:27–28; John 3:17; 1 Cor 6:9;
1 John 4:10). God forgives anyone and everyone when they trust Christ
as Savior (John 3:36; 6:40; 11:25–26; Titus 2:11–14; 1 John 1:9). Everyone
needs forgiveness in Christ (Luke 13:3; Rom 3:9–11), and everyone who
seeks forgiveness through Christ will find forgiveness (Rom 10:9–10, 13).

Christians are reconciled to God in Christ, and in Christ, all barriers
are broken down (Gal 3:28; Eph 2:14–15; Col 1:20). All the redeemed in
Christ are to live carrying the gospel of reconciliation to the world (Rom
5:10; 2 Cor 5:18–21). Therefore, impartial justice unifies all humans because it includes the truth that all humans are created in God's image, intrinsically equal (Gen 1:26–27), loved by God (John 3:16), personally sinful
before God, and in need of redemption (Rom 3:23), as well as the fact that
God desires for everyone to be redeemed (Matt 11:28–30). Once saved, we
also share in the same mandate to carry the message of reconciliation to the
world (Matt 28:18–20; 2 Cor 5:18–21).

Social justice is the work of the flesh, "enmities, strife, jealousy, out-
bursts of anger, disputes, dissensions, factions, envying" (Gal 5:19–21),
whereas the works of God's equal and impartial justice are "love, joy, peace,
patience, kindness, goodness, faithfulness, gentleness, self-control" (Gal
5:22–23). Christians are to reflect God's impartial love and justice toward
everyone (Exod 23:3; Lev 19:15; Mic 6:8) and compassionately minister to
the genuinely needy, the orphans, and the poor (Deut 10:18; Ps 140:12; 1
Tim 5:3; Jas 1:27) while maintaining that those who can work must work or
not eat (1 Thess 4:11; 2 Thess 3:10).

Unlike social justice, impartial justice guides us to obey the government (Rom 13:1–7), not to focus on retaliation (1 Pet 2:23) or reparations
or punishment for wrongs done in the past by others to our ancestors (1
Cor 13:5), but instead to focus on loving our neighbor as ourselves (Matt
22:39), praying for our enemies (Matt 5:10–12, 44), and developing Christ's
character in us (2 Pet 1:5–7) so we can share with all (Matt 19:19).

13

Racial Reconciliation Is Not the Gospel

A Critique of Dr. Jarvis Williams's Gospel

In the book *Removing the Stain of Racism from the Southern Baptist Convention,* Dr. Jarvis J. Williams contributes a chapter entitled, "Biblical Steps Toward Removing the Stain of Racism from the Southern Baptist Convention."

That he is a scholar is evident in his chapter. I did find myself in agreement with some things he said and parts of his "fifteen concluding exhortations related to removing the stain of racism from the SBC."[1] Although I will address his perspective on racism at another time, I do appreciate his acknowledgment that some progress has been made regarding race relations in the SBC.[2]

In this chapter, however, I am addressing his attempt to tie racial reconciliation too closely to the gospel of salvation. He conflates the message of the preached gospel by which people believe unto salvation with the gospel's accomplishments, effects, and consequences, many of which relate to becoming a new creation in Christ through regeneration and living out our faith (John 3:3–8; 2 Cor 5:17).

Some who desire to exalt the gospel attempt to expand it so that the totality of God's redemptive plan becomes the gospel; everything becomes Hmm. a gospel issue. But since it is impossible to include every salvific truth in the gospel definitionally, they usually focus on things such as social needs,

---

1. Williams and Jones, *Removing the Stain,* 45–51.
2. Williams and Jones, *Removing the Stain,* 44.

justice, social justice, or in Dr. Williams's case, racial reconciliation. This un-warranted expansion transfers biblical concepts that are associated with the Christian life such as loving our neighbor (Matt 22:39), the Holy Spirit-filled life (Gal 5:22–26) or imitating God (Eph 5:1) to the definition of the gospel.

It confuses what happens and what should happen in the saved person's life with the gospel we preach when we proclaim the good news of justification by faith in Jesus Christ, who is "the Lamb of God who takes away the sin of the world" (John 1:29). This attachment of the fruit of the gospel with the gospel message of God's sacrifice for us that we preach (John 3:16) unnecessarily complicates the gospel that leads to salvation by making results of the gospel requirements of the gospel. Results of the gospel such as receiving spiritual gifts, having and expressing desires and actions of Christians, loving each other, belonging to a local church, racial reconciliation, or any of countless other features designated in the New Testament as Christian responsibilities and blessing follow the reception of the gospel; therefore, they are not the gospel.

We see this same complication when people see the biblical gospel as too simple or when they desire to include elements of beliefs they deem important. Some in the church of Galatia were adding aspects of Judaism to the gospel (Gal 1:4–8). In more modern times, and out of the desire by many Christians to right the wrongs of society, various additions also have been made. For example, the Social Gospel movement flourished between 1870 and 1920. "Advocates of the movement interpreted the kingdom of God as requiring social as well as individual salvation."[3] Similarly, today we have the "justice gospel" or the "social justice gospel," which rightfully laments the injustices of society, but does so wrongfully through incorporating these non-salvific issues (some of which are actually components of cultural Marxism) into the simple gospel.

For Williams, it is a matter of racial reconciliation. He insists that we need to "advance the gospel of reconciliation and to erase the stain of racism from our denomination."[4] In Galatians, Judaizers corrupted the gospel by adding commandments and traditions from the Old Testament. Today, it is the addition of correcting various social ills by adding justice or in Williams's case, "the gospel of reconciliation," through ideas such as the gospel of justice. While some who promote these gospel add-ons may have dastardly motives, I assume most do not. They only, as a Christ-follower,

3. "Social Gospel," para. 1.
4. Williams and Jones, *Removing the Stain*, 46.

desire to make society a more just society as all Christians should, but it is unscriptural to bind their message too closely to the gospel of Christ.

It is a perilous mistake to make outcomes and blessings of the gospel identical to the gospel that we share that leads to salvation if one believes (1 Cor 15:1-4). If everything in Scripture, or said in Scripture to and for Christians, is the gospel, then what are we to make of progressive sanctification, discipleship, maturing, equipping, and the fruits of the Spirit? And what about the commands directed only to Christians and the instructions given only to Christians that are not necessary to do or even know about to be saved? All of the epistles and the book of Revelation were written to or for local churches, which are to be composed of people who have accepted the gospel and are now dedicated to learn and live the Scripture out in its fullest, something no unsaved person can do.

One passage Williams relies on to argue for the "gospel of reconciliation" is Ephesians 1:2-13. I have studied this passage many times and read numerous commentaries on it by both Calvinists and Extensivists (non-Calvinists). I see each perspective's particular emphases *explicitly* in the very words of the passage, and therefore I understand why each side argues their viewpoint. Williams is the first I have read that suggests, based on the passage, that the gospel is incomplete without racial reconciliation.

It is true that God's total work of salvation and "the summing up of all things in Christ" (vs. 10) includes the elimination of every barrier (theological, racial, economic, cultural, to name a few). But I challenge Williams's insistence that racial reconciliation is a part of the gospel we proclaim because it is included in "the summing up of all things in Christ." He inextricably connects salvation and racial reconciliation as essential components of the gospel by what he calls "entry language" and "maintenance language."[5]

Williams uses the Old Testament (LXX, the Greek translation of the Old Testament) and pagan literature usage of the terms *euaggelion* and *euaggelizo* (noun and verb forms of gospel) to support his contention. He also relies heavily on the reality that the gospel means good news and the fact that the term is used etymologically (etymology explains the origin and development of a word) to refer to various types of good news as being supportive of his attaching reconciliation to the gospel (Joel 2:18—3:2; Nah 1:8-14; 2:1—3:19; Isa 40:9; 52:7; 60:6; 61:1).

---

5. Williams and Jones, *Removing the Stain*, 30-31, 42.

Williams says, "As I stated above, evangelicals in general and Southern Baptists in particular often narrowly (and wrongly!) define gospel only in terms of entry language (i.e., how one becomes a Christian). But the gospel is broader than some are willing to admit. It includes both entry language (how one becomes a Christian) and maintenance language (how one lives in Spirit-empowered obedience)."[6] When he makes the gospel we preach include entry and maintenance language (the latter supposedly justifying making racial reconciliation a part of the gospel), he conflates the effects of the gospel with the evangelistic message, the gospel definitionally, which must be believed to be saved. Which raises the question, why this one aspect of racial reconciliation, and not other countless results of the gospel? Why not such things as being pro-life or stamping out poverty?

Paul says of the gospel he preached, "Now I make known to you, brethren, the gospel which I preached to you, which also you received, in which also you stand, by which also you are saved, if you hold fast the word which I preached to you, unless you believed in vain. For I delivered to you as of first importance what I also received, that Christ died for our sins according to the Scriptures, and that He was buried, and that He was raised on the third day according to the Scriptures" (1 Cor 15:1–4). Issues such as marital problems, actual social injustices, and the need for truth can be elements of illustrating our sinfulness before God by contextualizing the need for the gospel, but they are not, thereby, the gospel.

Williams also employs passages saying, "*Euaggelion* appears numerous times in Galatians to refer to the announcement about Jesus" (Gal 6:7, 11; 2:2, 5, 7, 14).[7] For the record, the gospel is intrinsically about Jesus's person and work to procure salvation and freely give to all who believe.

---

6. Williams and Jones, *Removing the Stain*, 42. This is the distinction he makes in his defense of making racial reconciliation's relationship to the gospel more than a result of the gospel. One might be inclined to understand his term "maintenance language" to be referring to what the gospel accomplishes, the life to be lived after receiving the gospel— Spirit-filled life, Christian marriage, serving Christ, or acting justly and righteously. But if that were the case, the chapter would be pointless since it seems that all would agree with that. I think the only conclusion he leaves us is that he seeks to tie racial reconciliation to the gospel definitionally, what must be believed or what must be a part of the gospel we preach unto salvation. If that is not his point, he has been painfully unclear. The lack of clarity would lie solely with him since a clarifier or two would resolve the ambiguity. For example, he could say, I do not mean that racial reconciliation is in any way a part of the gospel definitionally, what must be preached or believed unto salvation, or what is demanded in the gospel. Alas, he does not, but he does categorize it as a "demand" of the gospel.

7. Williams and Jones, *Removing the Stain*, 32.

Jesus and his work are why there is a gospel and what the gospel is about, which includes our need for the gospel because we are hopelessly sinful on our own. Thus, I do not know how this supports moving racial reconciliation from a fruit of the gospel to an integral component of the gospel, like preaching the death, burial, and resurrection of Christ.

Williams argues against the gospel being limited to justification by faith. He says, "The noun "gospel" (*euaggelion)* and the verb "to announce the gospel/good news" (*euaggelizo)* should not be defined exclusively in terms of justification by faith."[8] My response is if we are referring to what the gospel broadly accomplishes, then yes, he is correct. But when used as a climactic encapsulation of what the gospel is and does, which is the way it is commonly used, it is a wonderful explanation. The gospel is the incomparably good news that accomplishes a myriad of things that fall within the truth that by faith, the ungodly can be accepted by the holy God and declared to be eternally justified, and, therefore, without guilt. All of this is based on receiving the benefit of the atonement of Christ through faith; to wit, we are justified by faith.

Williams does admit, in reference to Galatians, that "Paul indicates that the gospel and the announcement of the good news in Galatia includes justification by faith . . . The gospel in Galatians should not be defined only as justification by faith—though Galatians teaches justification is part (an important part) of Paul's gospel."[9] Therefore, we see it as "an important part" but not a central message. Williams did not answer whether it was more, less, or held to be of the same importance as racial reconciliation.

After the first quote cited above, he goes into the etymology of the word, demonstrating how it meant various ideas of good news conveyed by the term in pagan literature and the LXX.[10] Which, as far as I can tell, does nothing to demonstrate that the gospel definitionally includes racial reconciliation in the message to believe unto salvation, nor that we should not find the apex of the gospel in "justification by faith." Donald K. Campbell says the purpose of Galatians was to address "the Judaizers in Galatia [who] both discredited Paul and proclaimed a false gospel . . . Paul contended for the true doctrine of grace, that is, for justification by faith alone."[11]

8. Williams and Jones, *Removing the Stain*, 31.

9. Williams and Jones, *Removing the Stain*, 36.

10. Williams and Jones, *Removing the Stain*, 31, 32–33 respectively.

11. Campbell outlines Galatians thusly, "It was necessary that Paul vindicate his apostleship and message, a task he undertook in the first two chapters. In this autobiographical

Williams spends considerable time arguing for an expanded understanding of the term gospel in order to defend his position on racial reconciliation. He draws on the usage of the verb and noun forms of gospel not
only from pagan sources but also from the book of Isaiah. Regarding the
book of Galatians, Williams says, "as they heard this letter read in a worship context, I do not believe they thought Paul was referencing only a turn
from justification by faith to a false gospel. Their understanding . . . would
have included justification by faith as well as . . . the other gospel/salva-
tion themes occurring in the letter that parallels Isaiah 40–66 and Genesis
12–50. Paul likely proclaimed these themes to them during his visit with
them (Acts 13:13—14:23; Gal 5:20–21)."[12]

Although Paul had been with the Galatians previously, being pagans
with little or no knowledge of the Old Testament, they would probably not
have linked the things Paul was condemning and correcting with Isaiah.
Rarely will you find a congregation today that can link them, even if they
have been taught the Old Testament. At best, I think it is highly speculative
to use that possibility in an attempt to justify his premise that racial reconciliation is a part of the gospel presentation. Williams's understanding of
the gospel we are to preach is so complicated and encumbered by conflating results of the gospel with the essentials of the gospel that he makes it
difficult to define the gospel succinctly and clearly. This difficulty is particularly true when we consider scores of other accomplishments and blessings
flowing from the gospel that we could add to his.

What about people who think the gospel should include some other
consequence or matter of justice instead of racial reconciliation? Each person mixing their particular emphases leaves the church with an unclear
universal gospel. What must I include in the gospel beyond belief in Christ
who died, was buried, and rose again to pay for the sins of the world (John
1:29) so that anyone and everyone can be forgiven of their sins so that God
is just in declaring them justified (John 3:16–18; Rom 3:24, 26). Nothing, if

section Paul demonstrated convincingly that his apostleship and his message came by
revelation from the risen Christ. In chapters 3 and 4 Paul contended for the true doctrine
of grace, that is, for justification by faith alone. Finally, to show that Christian liberty does
not mean license the apostle, in chapters 5 and 6, taught that a Christian should live by
the power of the Holy Spirit and that when he does he manifests in his life not the works
of the flesh but the fruit of the Spirit. Galatians was written to remedy a desperate situation, to call early Christians back from the Mosaic Law to grace, from legalism to faith. It
is an emphatic statement of salvation by faith apart from works and is as relevant today
as when it was originally penned." Campbell, "Galatians," 588.

12. Williams and Jones, *Removing the Stain*, 36–37.

we leave the gospel as found in Scripture. To add *anything* to that gospel is a corruption of consequence!

Justification, wherein God declares the ungodly who trust Christ as Savior to be justified in his sight, is the apex of salvation. James Leo Garrett Jr. states, "The condition of justification is faith in Christ (Gal 2:16a; 3:8a, 24; Rom 3:26, 28). The blessings issuing from justification include 'peace with God,' 'access' to God's 'grace,' joy and hope (Rom 5:1-2)."[13] By trusting the message of the gospel, God declares believers to be justified before him. And, blessings flow from that declaration.

Lewis Sperry Chafer explains justification like this: "No present position in which the believer is placed is more exalted and consummating than that of being justified by God. By justification, the saved one is lifted . . . to the estate of one whom God has declared justified forever, which estate the holy justice of God is as much committed to defend as ever that holy justice was before committed to condemn."[14] To think that is accomplished by the pure and simple gospel is immeasurably glorious and recognizes Christ's sacrifice and properly exalts him before the earth and angels. It is evident that to be in such a state would entail every other blessing from the gospel (including racial reconciliation) without them having to be a definitional component of the gospel believed.

Chafer further clarifies justification, saying, "The believer is constituted righteous by virtue of his position in Christ, but he is justified by a declaratory decree of God. Righteousness imputed is the abiding fact, and justification is the divine recognition of that fact."[15] Paul says, "Even the righteousness of God through faith in Jesus Christ for all those who believe; for there is no distinction" (Rom 3:22). By faith in Christ, we become righteous, and the Father confirms that by declaring us justified. Our faith results in the ungodly being declared righteous by God, who justifies us (Rom 4:5; see also Rom 3:24, 26; 5:18). Because we are justified by faith in Christ, we have peace with God. Paul says, "Therefore, having been justified by faith, we have peace with God through our Lord Jesus Christ" (Rom 5:1). Williams's contention that the gospel is only complete if it includes racial reconciliation as an essential component corrupts the gospel.

Williams does not indicate that he is arguing for racial reconciliation being a part of the gospel, broadly speaking, like spiritual gifts or the Holy

13. Garrett, *Systematic Theology*, 2:290.

14. Chafer, *Systematic Theology*, 3:245–46.

15. Chafer, *Systematic Theology*, 3:246.

Spirit-filled life, because that seems indisputable. Instead, he seems to be arguing for it as a part of the requirement of the gospel. For example, in arguing against racial reconciliation being merely a "social issue" or an implication of the gospel, he rejects ideas that make racial reconciliation something that is "not part of the gospel's *demand*"[16] (italics added). The demand of the gospel is not something that is included or resulting from believing the gospel, but rather it gives every indication of being a demand like the demand of the gospel to believe in Christ for the saving of a person's soul.

I agree with Williams's contention that racial reconciliation is not merely a social issue for Christians because it is also a moral problem. That being said, I do not believe it is a part of the gospel's "demand" as when Christ said, "Those beside the road are those who have heard; then the devil comes and takes away *the word* from their heart, so that they will not believe and be saved" (Luke 8:12; see also John 3:18; Rom 10:9–11). *The word* taken away, which is the gospel, means that the opportunity of salvation is gone. This belief is a very specific belief in Christ, regardless if a person has ever heard of racial reconciliation. As Peter made clear in his Pentecost message, "And it shall be that everyone who calls on the name of the Lord will be saved" (Acts 2:21). Again, Williams confuses results and blessings of the gospel with the explicit message and requirement—demand—of the gospel; the essence of what must be preached and believed for someone to be saved is the gospel. But Williams makes racial reconciliation a part of the gospel we proclaim if we are to preach the gospel of Christ and as Christ did.

For example, he uses Matthew 15:21–28 to demonstrate that Christ preached racial reconciliation as a part of the gospel. He says, "In essence, Jesus preached racial reconciliation as part of his gospel message."[17] I believe if a person is just examining the text, he will find matters such as God's timing was Israel first, and the gentiles would be included later. It was not time for him to bring blessing to the gentiles. The narrative forthrightly depicts the Canaanite woman seeing herself not as one of the family (deserving of his help, food), but as a dog, thereby demonstrating her great humility and faith. Then, even though he was "sent only to the lost sheep

---

16. Williams is arguing against Randy White and other Christians who make it either merely a social issue or "an implication of the gospel." Williams and Jones, *Removing the Stain*, 29.

17. Williams and Jones, *Removing the Stain*, 30.

of the house of Israel" (vs. 24), and salvation is to the Jew first (Rom 1:16), Christ responds to her faith.

She demonstrated the very humility and faith that he sought to find in the house of Israel. His response showed that the time was near for whoever exercised such faith would be his people, which is the hope of the gentiles who did not have the law (John 3:16). She exercised the faith and humility he desired to see among the Jewish leaders who had the law but rejected him. Such hope for the gentiles to be saved by faith is obscured or diminished when someone imposes racial reconciliation or other opinions about social justice as an inherent part of the gospel Jesus preached.

Christ was not emphasizing racial reconciliation, but illustrating a time was coming in which Jew and gentile will come to him by faith alone. The racial reconciliation that would occur is because of the power of the gospel to save so that all who believe are justified; all stand on equal footing before the cross. If we leave racial reconciliation where countless other blessings are, it is not diminished any more than the rest of the results that come from the transforming power of the gospel, one of which is that Christians are one (Gal 3:26–29). It should be noted that the passage does mention the things I mentioned, but it does not mention racial reconciliation. Further, when results of the gospel are inextricably integrated into the demand of the gospel we preach whereby the ungodly are justified by faith, we complicate and distort the saving gospel.

Williams, as others do, confuses the definition of the gospel with the applicatory consequences of the gospel. After concluding that Jesus's preaching included racial reconciliation as a "part of his gospel,"[18] he says at the bottom of that page, "Southern Baptists need to develop a biblical theology of the gospel . . . they must be committed to the *whole* gospel"[19] (italics added). That can only mean Southern Baptists have been preaching a partial, incomplete gospel because we did not make racial reconciliation an essential part of the saving gospel.

He continues, saying, "The gospel includes both entry language (repentance and faith, justification by faith and reconciliation with God [Rom 3:21—5:11; 1 Cor 15:1–8], etc.) and maintenance language (walking in the Spirit [Gal 5:16–26], reconciliation between Jews and Gentiles [Eph 2:11—3:8], and loving one another in the power of the Spirit [Gal

---

18. Williams and Jones, *Removing the Stain*, 30.

19. Williams and Jones, *Removing the Stain*, 30.

5:13–14; 6:1–2])."[20] First, these categories provide his framework for making racial reconciliation a definitional part of the gospel message like repentance and faith.

Second, it should be obvious that such an inclusion strongly indicates that he does not view racial reconciliation in a resultant manner, but instead as an integral part of the presented gospel because no one is arguing it is not a result of believing the gospel. To wit, it is both a blessing and a challenge to all Christians. Third, at a minimum, his position raises the serious question of how it is to be presented in the sharing of the gospel. Must it be accepted along with faith in Christ (remember he said he rejects positions where it is "not part of the gospel's demand"), and what if it is not included? Maybe the last point is clarified by his statement that "Southern Baptists . . . must be committed to the whole gospel."

This statement, along with his certainty that Jesus "preached racial reconciliation as a part of his gospel message," leads to the fundamental question of whether Southern Baptists have been committed to the whole gospel or not. If we have, then he stands with many before him who sought to add something that does not belong to the gospel "demand." At least he is making the simple gospel unnecessarily more complex and, therefore, more complicated, which warps the gospel.

Fourth, why pick racial reconciliation as the only social justice requirement of the gospel we preach unto salvation? Why not prison reform, eradicating homelessness, or the redistribution of wealth and power? As adamantly opposed as I am to the barbaric practice of killing babies prenatally and postnatally (abortion and infanticide), stopping the killing of babies is not a part of the gospel unto salvation, a demand of the gospel, and neither is racial reconciliation.

The gospel is the message we preach to the lost whereby they may be saved if they believe the gospel and damned if they do not. The lost are not commanded to walk in the Spirit (Gal 5:16–26), because only those who have received the gospel and been born again can do so. To walk in the Spirit requires that the Holy Spirit is living in the person, and the Holy Spirit is not given to people unless they accept the gospel. The Holy Spirit takes up residence in the believer, and one becomes a believer *after* accepting the gospel. Many things, like racial reconciliation in Christ, are dependent on having received the Holy Spirit, which only happens after the gospel is received.

20. Williams and Jones, *Removing the Stain*, 31.

We must always be clear. The gospel unto salvation that we preach results in countless blessings, but they are not required to be mentioned or understood, much less believed and experienced by the lost, to be saved. The gospel does not include the "demand" to include or accept *anything* about racial reconciliation, social justice, or even living the Spirit-filled life. The passages that speak of experiencing the blessings, results (1 Cor 1:5–7; Eph 1:3), and commands of the Christian life are said to Christians about the Christian life (Eph 4:1; 5:1–2).

What Williams calls maintenance language is really language reflective of what the lost receive when they accept the gospel and become Christians. It is the language of living out the new life, practical sanctification, maturing in the faith, faithfulness, and the Spirit-filled life. The new life is obtained by faith in the truth of the gospel that proclaims the death, burial, and resurrection of Jesus who paid for our sins (John 1:29; Heb 2:9; 10:10, 14). That salvation is available to all who believe in Christ and his finished work.

The effects, blessings, promises, and commands to Christians are not essential parts of the gospel that must be believed or preached for that matter. They are not definitionally the gospel. Racial reconciliation between believers was achieved on the cross and is applied when we are saved. We just have to recognize that fact and walk in it as we do other blessings of salvation (Eph 2:10–22). One has to notice that selecting any one of many results of the gospel and transforming them into requirements of the gospel not only confuses results with demands of the gospel but is entirely subjective. As I have maintained, why racial reconciliation and not one of the countless other blessings of the gospel?

Chafer lists thirty-three of what he rightly calls "riches of grace." He says these "together comprise the salvation of a soul . . . They are wrought of God; they are wrought instantaneously; they are wrought simultaneously; they are grounded on the merit of Christ; and being grounded on the merit of Christ, are eternal. It follows that each person of the human family at a given moment is either perfectly saved, being the recipient of every spiritual blessing in Christ Jesus, or perfectly lost, being without one of these spiritual blessings."[21]

While many of the great truths referred to by Chafer are a part of the gospel presentation of reconciliation to God (forgiveness of trespasses and justification), everything that is included in "every spiritual blessing" is not (Eph 1:3). That would include every present blessing and future blessing in

21. Chafer, *Systematic Theology*, 3:234. See the list of thirty-three on pages 234–65.

the rapture, millennial kingdom, and eternity. Notice Chafer says the lost do not have "one of these spiritual blessings," and the saved have "every spiritual blessing in Christ Jesus." They come to those in Christ, and being in Christ is our position after we believe the gospel unto salvation.

One of these blessings is our reconciliation to God (Rom 5:10; Rom 5:18) and other people (Eph 2:10–22). And the only path to true reconciliation of people to each other, including racial reconciliation, is the gospel of salvation, which does not include racial reconciliation definitionally or as a "demand," but rather as a consequence of salvation (Gal 5:18–26)—being able to love our neighbor as our self is dependent on first loving God (Matt 22:37–39). If we preach the gospel so that people are reconciled to God, we will have the power of God for racial reconciliation that Christ achieved on the cross (Eph 2:14–15). But racial reconciliation is neither a demand of the gospel to be accepted for salvation, nor is it a definitional part of the gospel except resultantly.

One should always keep in mind that the barrier between Jew and gentile is not merely about racial reconciliation or racism as thought of today in which one's relationship with God is not even a factor. Instead, it was how one could have a relationship with God that was the chief factor (far more than skin pigmentation or geographical location) that divided Jew and gentile. First, God chose to create the Jewish nation and covenant with them (Gen 12:1–3), and therefore the gentile, regardless of the color of his skin, was outside of that relationship and came to God by becoming a proselyte (Eph 2:11–12).[22]

After the cross, the problem between Jew and gentile was still not about race and reconciling them—ethnicity per se—as we think about it contemporarily or as Williams writes. The problem was not even whether gentiles could be saved because that was no mystery (something that was hidden in the past Gal 3:29; Eph 2:12–16; 3:3–6). Instead, it has always been that the cross means that Jew and gentile are saved the same way, by faith in Christ (Rom 3:22; 4:11, 16; 10:4). That is the issue of Galatians. That is what the Judaizers so diligently fought against. Therefore, again, we see the purity of the complete gospel is not about racial reconciliation but doctrinal reconciliation so that Jew and gentile stand on equal footing at the cross, and every person becomes a Christian the same way, by trusting the gospel of Jesus Christ.

---

22. Also known as a God-fearing gentile (Acts 13:43; 17:4).

It is a dangerously unbiblical decision to make racial reconciliation essential so that without it as a part of the gospel presentation, we fail to preach the "whole gospel" as Williams puts it. Clearly, he is not arguing for racial reconciliation to be a part of the gospel in a resultant or applicatory manner because that is clear, and I think most Biblicists gladly recognize that it is. If he were trying to make that point, he sought to do so in the most beclouded, circuitous, obfuscatory manner I have seen. But he is not so inept; he is a scholar and seeks to present a scholarly defense of the "gospel of racial reconciliation" as he puts it.[23]

The Statement on Social Justice & the Gospel provides a concise clarification of the gospel in the context of rejecting the addition of such things as social justice or racial reconciliation. It says,

> WE AFFIRM that the gospel is the divinely-revealed message concerning the person and work of Jesus Christ—especially his virgin birth, righteous life, substitutionary sacrifice, atoning death, and bodily resurrection—revealing who he is and what he has done with the promise that he will save anyone and everyone who turns from sin by trusting him as Lord.
>
> WE DENY that anything else, whether works to be performed or opinions to be held, can be added to the gospel without perverting it into another gospel. This also means that implications and applications of the gospel, such as the obligation to live justly in the world, though legitimate and important in their own right, are not definitional components of the gospel.[24]

I agree with this statement. Therefore, though racial reconciliation is vital as a result of the gospel, and accordingly to be modeled and promulgated by Christians, it is not a "definitional component of the gospel." Moreover, it is the preaching of the gospel of Jesus Christ that results in true and lasting racial reconciliation by leading individuals first to be reconciled to God (2 Cor 5:18–21).

Williams cites Ephesians 1:9–10, saying, "The Bible's categories of race and racial reconciliation intersect with its categories of salvation and gospel. Especially in Ephesians, the mystery of the gospel is defined as the unification of all things in Christ (Eph 1:9–10), which includes the reconciliation

---

23. Williams and Jones, *Removing the Stain*, 46.

24. The statement references the following Scriptures: Gen 3:15; Prov 29:18; Isa 25:7; 60:2, 3; Rom 1:16–17; 10:14, 15, 17; 1 Cor 15:1–11; Gal 1:6–9; Rev 13:8.

of Jews and Gentiles into 'one new humanity' (Eph 2:11—3:8 NIV)."[25] Well, of course, it "intersects" and is "included" in Christ since racial reconciliation is one of the "things in the heavens and on earth" (Eph 1:10; Col 1:16, 20), but that does not make it a definitional part of the gospel message. It does not make it anymore what is "demanded" than the galaxy of other accomplishments of the gospel "in the heavens and on earth" that are a part of the "summing up of all things in Christ" (Eph 1:10).

Louis A. Barbieri Jr. defines mysteries, saying, "New Testament 'Mysteries' (previously unknown, but now-revealed truths)."[26] Paul said the mystery in Ephesians 1 is the summing up of all things in Christ (v. 10), and in Ephesians 3:6, the mystery is that gentiles become fellow heirs with Jews in the same way as Jews become heirs, and that is by believing the gospel. The mystery hidden was not that gentiles could and would be saved, but they would be saved in the same way as Jews. They would not have to become a Jew, keep the law, or adopt any of Judaism's practices, but both Jew and gentile would be saved the same way, by faith alone (John 3:1–14; Rom 1:16–17). Gentiles become equal heirs. There are no second-class heirs.

Similarly, as with Ephesians 1:9–10, Williams includes Romans 1:16–17 as a passage about racial reconciliation, saying the verses "demonstrate that the Bible's categories of race and racial reconciliation intersect with its categories of salvation and gospel."[27] If he means by intersecting that they interrelate, then I agree, as I have said before, but that does not seem to be what he means.

The passage is not about racial reconciliation, even though that happens when the true gospel is preached and received. It is rather about the true gospel, which is received by faith and the same for everyone. The efficacy of the gospel is in the "power of God," which was sequentially given first to the Jews and then to the gentiles. God covenanted with the Jews in the Old Testament. They experienced a privileged position with God and received the law (Rom 3:1–2).

Now there is no advantage for the Jew. All hear the gospel and are saved by faith in Christ and his sacrificial death for the sins of the world (John 1:29). The gospel is not about racial justice (or any other form of social justice), but it is about God incarnate who died, was buried, and rose from the dead so that all people, races, can be justified and forgiven (Rom

---

25. Williams and Jones, *Removing the Stain*, 29.

26. Barbieri, "Matthew," 48.

27. Williams and Jones, *Removing the Stain*, 29.

4:25). The gospel is sufficient for all, and when we are saved, we are reconciled to God and man.

John A. Witmer, speaking of Paul's view of the gospel in this passage, said, "He identified it as the infinite resources (dynamis, 'spiritual ability') of God applied toward the goal of salvation in the life of everyone who believes regardless of racial background."[28] Thus, race intersects with the power of the gospel, but the power of the gospel is not about nor seen in racial reconciliation, reconciling man to man. But the power of the gospel is seen in its ability to reconcile anyone and everyone to God by faith alone, regardless of their sins, history, or race. The Jewish privilege was over (Rom 2:26).

Witmer further says regarding Paul,

> He recognized, however, a priority *for the Jew* expressed in the word *first*, which has sufficient textual support here and is unquestioned in 2:9-10. Because the Jews were God's Chosen People (11:1), the custodians of God's revelation (3:2), and the people through whom Christ came (9:5), they have a preference of privilege expressed historically in a chronological priority. As the Lord Jesus said, 'Salvation is from the Jews' (John 4:22). In Paul's ministry he sought out the Jews first in every new city (Acts 13:5, 14; 14:1; 17:2, 10, 17; 18:4, 19; 19:8). Three times he responded to their rejection of his message by turning to the Gentiles (Acts 13:46; 18:6; 28:25-28; cf. comments on Eph. 1:12). Today evangelism of the world must include the Jews, but the priority of the Jews has been fulfilled.[29]

Consequently, I agree that racial reconciliation is a part of the gospel in what it accomplishes or entails broadly speaking (Gal 3:28; Eph 2:10-22; 3:6; 4:3-6). That is to say, in salvation, all barriers between Jew and gentile, those having the law and those not having the law, are broken down, and we are one body of believers. Therefore, reconciliation has been achieved for all the redeemed. We must recognize it and walk in it, but we do not have to achieve it, and it does intersect with the gospel in that it is a result of what Christ has accomplished for us. Williams errs grievously by tethering racial reconciliation *too* closely to the gospel of salvation's presentation and requirements. If that is not his intent, he could have easily said so.

Williams references several LXX verses which contain the word gospel (in the noun *euaggelion* and the verb form *euaggelizo*) and says,

28. Witmer, "Romans," 441.

29. Witmer, "Romans," 441.

In summary, in each of the above examples, *euaggelizo* is connected with the announcement of the Lord's mercy or salvation, and the Lord himself is present in the announcement. This means the heralds of the announcement . . . also proclaim the Lord himself. When the gospel of the Lord is announced, the Lord himself is present in the announcement in order to effect both the salvation and the judgment the announcement proclaims. Thus, the verb *euaggelizo* refers to the act of announcing the message of salvation and judgment in the LXX. The noun *euaggelion* refers to the content of the announcement.[30]

I do not see how this bolsters his case for including racial reconciliation as a definitional component of the gospel. Because, of course, Christ is there with us presenting the gospel (Matt 28:18–20). The gospel is all about Christ in such a way that if he were not alive and present, there would be no gospel (John 3:18). But specifically, the gospel is a proclamation of his atonement for sin, and how one is saved, which necessarily presupposes we have sinned and are sinners.

To not make racial reconciliation inherent in the gospel message, what is said or must be accepted for salvation, makes it no less a part of the salvation plan of God than any of the other effects and blessings of the gospel. It merely changes the sequential order in which it occurs. Instead of being a part of the gospel *definitionally* (as Williams seems to demand), it is a part of the gospel's accomplishment. Accordingly, justice is not part of the definition or proclamation of the gospel unto salvation (to be believed), but it is a part of the Christian life's demand.

Williams repeatedly uses verses that do not explicitly talk about racial reconciliation, particularly in the way it is used in his chapter. But these verses do explicitly mention other aspects of the gospel (Rom 1:16–17; Gal 2:13). For example, Galatians 2:11–14 is not about race per se as the term is currently used in society, in Williams's chapter, or the book where it is about racial reconciliation as an end in and of itself—with or without doctrine. It was not dealing with the Jews rejecting gentiles or vice-versa merely because of race or skin color; it was most importantly about their beliefs.

Regarding Peter's failure to walk in the true gospel that resulted in the rebuke from Paul, Williams says, "Peter failed to walk in the truth of the gospel when he withdrew from table fellowship with Gentile Christians, for fear of the Jews . . . Peter believed all the right things about justification

---

30. Williams and Jones, *Removing the Stain*, 34.

by faith for Jews, but he departed from the gospel by imposing Jewish legal demands on Gentile Scripture. His error stemmed from an incorrect view of the gospel's horizontal component."[31]

While I understand that Peter imposing Torah requirements on gentiles was mistaken, I believe Williams is wrong to make this merely a horizontal—racial—issue. The problem is that according to the gospel, it is a perversion to impose Jewish tradition (or racial reconciliation) on anyone because both Jew and gentile are saved by faith alone; that is the message of Galatians. Consequently, this was not an error regarding "the gospel's horizontal component." It was an error cutting to the very core of the gospel itself, and, therefore, promoting a false gospel.[32] Paul spoke of a specific situation that had arisen, but keep in mind that the wrong gospel for the gentiles is the wrong gospel for the Jews since there is only one gospel.

Williams seems to be trying to show that the problem was merely a horizontal issue so that he can justify requiring racial reconciliation as a part of the gospel. Peter clearly was adding to justification by faith alone, but that is not the same as being lost. One can err and still be saved. It is, in fact, the message of justification by faith that Judaizers were corrupting by imposing legalism on Christian liberty. Peter's actions were not just horizontal or between races, but vertical in that his actions obscured or denied the essence of the gospel, which is justification by faith for everyone.

Any recognition of Jews keeping the law was a corruption of the gospel, and imposing such on gentiles was a corruption as well. It was not merely a horizontal issue. It was not a failure to understand the racial problems needing racial reconciliation or social justice. Peter needed to get back to the true and only gospel, which is salvation by faith alone for everyone. Any understanding of the gospel, including Peter's misrepresentation that adds anything to it or modifies it for any particular group, is a vertical issue of the utmost importance because it creates a false gospel.

Williams says, "Of course, for an exhaustive definition of the gospel, one must look at the whole Bible . . . But may what I have put forth above put to rest once and for all one-sided, incomplete, and misleading definitions of the gospel."[33] Again, he conflates what the gospel results in, God's salvation plan from Genesis 3:15 to eternity, with the gospel we present unto salvation through faith, which does not include everything, nor even

31. Williams and Jones, *Removing the Stain*, 37.
32. Williams and Jones, *Removing the Stain*, 37.
33. Williams and Jones, *Removing the Stain*, 39.

many or most things, entailed in what the gospel accomplishes; nor can it. Everything in Scripture is not the gospel. Every story in Scripture is not the gospel. They may all point to, prepare for, or result from the gospel, but not everything in Scripture is the gospel; nor can it be. Teaching on such people as Noah, Abraham, and Sarah, and such areas as marriage, family, giving, and work ethics are not the gospel. To preach the gospel and to believe the gospel unto salvation does not mean a person has to believe in racial reconciliation (or even know whether there is such a feature) or a host of other items to be faithful in proclaiming the whole gospel or to be saved.

The confrontation was about Peter corrupting the "truth of the gospel" (vs.14) by seeking to mix the law and grace. In Antioch, Peter ate and fellowshiped with gentiles, which was in keeping with the gospel and the vision he had (Acts 10:10–16). This behavior was a testimony to the truth of the gospel, that Jew and gentile are saved the same way by faith alone; there is one body. As a result of this truth, gentiles did not need to add the law to the gospel, but neither did the Judaizers, much less require it of others. Both were corruptions of the gospel because the law is not a part of salvation for either Jew or gentile.

The Judaizers were wrong to add the law and were wrong to demand the gentiles do so. Notice, the passage is not about racial reconciliation but the nature of the gospel, which is the same for all. To make Peter's corruption analogous to promoting racial reconciliation seems to necessitate that either blacks or whites (or some other race) are teaching that some are saved differently than by faith alone. Then it would be analogous in that it requires a doctrinal reconciliation as the means of promoting the true gospel.

Peter's actions, like the Judaizers, were in effect saying there are two bodies of Christ, and that the Judaizers were correct in adding to the gospel and requiring the same of the gentiles. This changed the gospel so that they could not be saved apart from adopting some of the law, dietary restrictions, and circumcision like the Judaizers. Peter had defended the gospel and the preaching of it to the gentiles before the Jerusalem leaders (Acts 11:18) but was now creating a division in the gospel out of *fear* (v. 12). Consequently, while racial reconciliation was a part, the breach was a corruption of not merely race relations, but of the gospel itself so that it became another gospel. Not that Peter was necessarily changing his theology, but he was at least acting as though he was because of fear.

The effect of the Judaizers, which Peter was giving into, is that they were corrupting the gospel, not according to discordant racial relations as we think today, but by adding works of the law such as requiring circumcision. Campbell notes, "Further, the defectors were not acting according to the truth of the gospel, that is, they were denying by their actions the truth that on the basis of Jesus Christ's death and resurrection, Jews and Gentiles who believe are accepted equally by God."[34]

Therefore, the issue was not primarily racial reconciliation but doctrinal reconciliation. The Judaizers needed to fully embrace salvation by faith in Christ and his atoning work for Jew and gentile—the world—but they proclaimed another gospel. Correcting the doctrine of salvation, the gospel, would lead to racial reconciliation, but racial reconciliation would not necessarily lead to the doctrine of salvation, the gospel. Williams puts the cart before the horse.

Here are some thoughts on *why* we need the gospel, and how that *why* makes the gospel the good news; it clarifies what must be included in the gospel for it to be the good news from God we need to hear and believe.

The Need for the Gospel

Each person is headed for hell because he is a sinner.

- "For all have sinned and fall short of the glory of God" (Rom 3:23).

- "His winnowing fork is in His hand, and He will thoroughly clear His threshing floor; and He will gather His wheat into the barn, but He will burn up the chaff with unquenchable fire" (Matt 3:12).

- "Do not fear those who kill the body but are unable to kill the soul; but rather fear Him who is able to destroy both soul and body in hell" (Matt 10:28).

- "As it is written, 'There is none righteous, not even one; There is none who understands, There is none who seeks for God'" (Rom 3:10–11).

- "And if anyone's name was not found written in the book of life, he was thrown into the lake of fire" (Rev 20:15).

---

34. Campbell, "Galatians," 595.

Judgment Is Personal

God judges each person for his sin, and no one else's.

- "The person who sins will die. The son will not bear the punishment for the father's iniquity, nor will the father bear the punishment for the son's iniquity; the righteousness of the righteous will be upon himself, and the wickedness of the wicked will be upon himself. But if the wicked man turns from all his sins which he has committed and observes all My statutes and practices justice and righteousness, he shall surely live; he shall not die" (Ezek 18:20–21).

- "I tell you, no, but unless you repent, you will all likewise perish" (Luke 13:3).

The Basis for the Gospel

It is not because of what is in man, but because of what is in God. It is because of God's grace, mercy, and love of his creation.

- "For I have no pleasure in the death of anyone who dies," declares the Lord God. "Therefore, repent and live" (Ezek 18:32).

- "For the Son of Man did not come to destroy men's lives, but to save them" (Luke 9:56).

- "For the Son of Man has come to save that which was lost" (Matt 18:11).

Forgiveness Is for All

God salvationally loves every person.

- "The next day he saw Jesus coming to him and said, 'Behold, the Lamb of God who takes away the sin of the world'" (John 1:29).

- "You know that He appeared in order to take away sins; and in Him there is no sin" (1 John 3:5).

- "For the grace of God has appeared, bringing salvation to all men" (Titus 2:11).

The Gospel

What we say and what the lost must believe to be saved.

- "And that repentance for forgiveness of sins would be proclaimed in His name to all the nations, beginning from Jerusalem" (Luke 24:47).

- "But as many as received Him, to them He gave the right to become children of God, even to those who believe in His name" (John 1:12).

- "For God so loved the world, that He gave His only begotten Son, that whoever believes in Him shall not perish, but have eternal life" (John 3:16).

- "He who believes in Him is not judged; he who does not believe has been judged already, because he has not believed in the name of the only begotten Son of God" (John 3:18).

- "But these have been written so that you may believe that Jesus is the Christ, the Son of God; and that believing you may have life in His name" (John 20:31).

- "Of Him all the prophets bear witness that through His name everyone who believes in Him receives forgiveness of sins" (Acts 10:43).

- "And after he brought them out, he said, 'Sirs, what must I do to be saved?' They said, 'Believe in the Lord Jesus, and you will be saved, you and your household'" (Acts 16:30–31).

- "Therefore having overlooked the times of ignorance, God is now declaring to men that all people everywhere should repent, because He has fixed a day in which He will judge the world in righteousness through a Man whom He has appointed, having furnished proof to all men by raising Him from the dead" (Acts 17:30–31).

- "For I am not ashamed of the gospel, for it is the power of God for salvation to everyone who believes, to the Jew first and also to the Greek. For in it the righteousness of God is revealed from faith to faith; as it is written, "BUT THE RIGHTEOUS *man* SHALL LIVE BY FAITH" (Rom 1:16–17).

- "Now I make known to you, brethren, the gospel which I preached to you, which also you received, in which also you stand, by which also you are saved, if you hold fast the word which I preached to you, unless you believed in vain. For I delivered to you as of first importance what I also received, that Christ died for our sins according to the Scriptures, and that He was buried, and that He was raised on the third day according to the Scriptures" (1 Cor 15:1–4).

- "Now all these things are from God, who reconciled us to Himself through Christ and gave us the ministry of reconciliation, namely, that God was in Christ reconciling the world to Himself, not counting their trespasses against them, and He has committed to us the word of reconciliation. Therefore, we are ambassadors for Christ, as though God were making an appeal through us; we beg you on behalf of Christ, be reconciled to God. He made Him who knew no sin to be sin on our behalf, so that we might become the righteousness of God in Him" (2 Cor 5:18–21).

- "For by grace you have been saved through faith; and that not of yourselves, it is the gift of God" (Eph 2:8).

- For the grace of God has appeared, bringing salvation to all men" (Titus 2:11).

- "And He Himself is the propitiation for our sins; and not for ours only, but also for those of the whole world" (1 John 2:2).

- "By this the love of God was manifested in us, that God has sent His only begotten Son into the world so that we might live through Him" (1 John 4:9).

The message of the gospel answers the question of the evangelist, "What message do I share with people so that they may be reconciled to God, have sins forgiven, and have eternal life?" The gospel answers the question of the lost whom we evangelize, "What must I do to be saved?" (1 Cor 15:1–4). Williams attempts to incorporate racial reconciliation (social justice) with that simple gospel message and, therefore, corrupts the gospel.

The gospel unto salvation does not include any components of the law such as circumcision or dietary restrictions, opinions about social justice, acts of social justice, or racial reconciliation; all such additions corrupt the gospel into another gospel, which is really not another gospel. Thus, it is a corruption of consequence. The gospel unto salvation is about the person and work of Christ paying for our sins and freely offering sinners the way to be justified by faith because of his finished work of salvation (Rom 10:8–13).

Although every person who accepts the gospel receives all that is accomplished by Christ and his salvific work such as the sanctified life, spiritual gifts, answered prayer, results emanating from regenerated lives upon society, understanding of true justice, and the ability to apply God's justice to society and all other relationships, these are *not* the gospel. One neither needs to understand, do, or even know such will happen to be saved. These are the accomplishments and blessings of the gospel.

Williams and others tragically blur these lines by conflating results of the gospel with the gospel and thereby corrupt the pure and simple gospel. Any addition is unnecessary, corruptive, and subjective. One may easily see the subjectivity of such additions by considering the myriad of options one could choose from their particular interest or past (like in Galatians). Or one could choose from among issues he finds very important like Williams does in racial reconciliation and social justice (social justice as used today is not the same as biblical justice, and, therefore, is not even a result of the gospel).[35]

Williams says, "One should see that Paul and Isaiah offer many components of the gospel."[36] But as I have argued, these components are not essential to the message of the gospel that answers, "What must I do to be saved?" He simply and repeatedly confuses attendant blessings, components, and consequences of the gospel as entailed in the whole plan of salvation, justification, sanctification, and glorification, now and forever, with the gospel proper.

Of course, the Old Testament is the fountainhead of the New Testament, including the gospel and justification, but hearing or understanding the Old Testament is not essential to be saved, and therefore be justified.[37] Although the redemptive work of Christ includes many matters prophesied about and portrayed in the Old Testament (such as types and prophecies), it is not essential to understand all of them to be saved, least of all any kind of racial reconciliation.

---

35. Dr. Larry Toothaker provides an easy way to understand the problem. He says, "We could line up 100 Christians, each of whom could add their requirement to be added to the gospel. Person one says it is to be pro-life, person two says it is to include racial reconciliation; person three says it is to feed the poor. And then we would have 100 gospels, not just one. But the last man asks, 'What must I do to be saved?' Which of the 100 do we tell him?" He made this comment to me and is a member of my church.

36. Williams and Jones, *Removing the Stain*, 35.

37. Geisler, *Systematic Theology*, 3:235.

A Corruption of Consequence

Norman Geisler reminds us that "The heart cry of the Reformation was 'justification by faith alone!'"[38] Campbell notes, "Galatians . . . played such a key role in the Reformation that it was called 'the cornerstone of the Protestant Reformation.' This was because its emphasis on salvation by grace through faith alone was the major theme of the preaching of the Reformers. Luther was especially attached to Galatians and referred to it as his wife. He lectured on the book extensively, and his commentary on Galatians was widely read by the common people."[39]

Campbell reminds us of its influence even today. He says, "The profound influence of this small epistle continues. It is indeed the 'Magna Carta of Christian Liberty,' proclaiming to modern generations that salvation from the penalty and power of sin comes not by works but by grace through faith in God's provision."[40] Galatians' emphasis on salvation by faith positions it as second only to Romans, with Romans being more thorough. Although I do not doubt Williams's character, sincerity, or love for the gospel, I believe his attempt to bind racial reconciliation to the gospel of salvation by faith in the manner he does it is unwarranted and corruptive to the gospel. It is a corruption of consequence.

38. Geisler, Norman. *Systematic Theology,* vol. 3, 235.
39. Campbell, "Galatians," 587.
40. Campbell, "Galatians," 587.

Appendix 1

Why Defunding the Police is Destructive to Civil Society

- *It ignores the cries of all the innocents*: I stand against all injustices. Many who seek the defunding of police departments because of an injustice done by officers' handling of George Floyd do so by inflicting (or approving of such) injustices on countless innocent lives and their livelihoods. Something from which they will never recover. We must not even tacitly countenance such unjustness.

- *It entrusts public safety to anarchists*: Our local deliberations cannot be isolated from the pressures wrought by those who have strewn unlawful, heinous barbarism against innocent, law-abiding citizens across our land. Their propagation of anarchical terrorism to get their way proves they cannot be trusted to protect our society; therefore, we need the police now more than ever, and the police need our vocal support.

- *It wantonly penalizes every respectable police officer*: To establish such a pattern is to sanction inequality, which is the very thing civil societies seek to eliminate.

- *It violates reason*: Neither common sense nor statistical research supports the notion that the police are needed less in the day in which we live than yesterday. Nor is there evidence to support that systemic racism plagues our police departments; this does not suggest there are not some racist police officers as there may be individual racists in other professions. To portray the problem various cultures experience as caused by systemic racism is to ignore and thereby perpetuate the actual issues like the systemic breakdown of the family, the systemic blaming of black crime on racism or the legacy of slavery, demeaning of black Americans by the perpetuation of the welfare state, and the fight by the NAACP and the NEA against school choice. To hear the counterarguments to claims of systemic racism being the problem, I encourage you to read and listen to black intellectuals and scholars such as Thomas Sowell, Walter Williams, Robert L. Woodson Sr., Shelby Steele, and Larry Elder.[1]

- *It erects a faulty trajectory:* It is neither moral nor reasonable to deal with an immoral police officer by penalizing all police officers. It is as flawed as it would be to defund education of all students because of some bad students or punish all doctors, preachers, and even city council representatives because of a rogue member. To dismiss this reason because one thinks the scenario we are embroiled in cannot be expanded to include our own vocations or affect a person's ability to serve in public life safely is actually to give evidence for this point.

- *It undermines consensual politics:* To either defund or reduce police departments' budgets in a climate of fear emanating from protests that either may or do turn into anarchical riots encourages more of the same by more groups over more issues. Anarchists are emboldened and are not satisfied for the long-term by such concessions.

- *It discriminates against every law-abiding citizen:* Every law-abiding citizen who is grateful for our police and the job they do daily deserves police protection. The notion that we need to decrease that protection is contrary to reality.

- *It is an acquiescence to fear:* This is not a denial of the misuse of power by some police officers, rather it is to argue that the facts do not back up a claim that police departments generally, and the Norman Police Department specifically, suffer from systemic racism or epidemic corruption or deserve a reduction in funding.[2]

1. I refer to men like these as "black intellectuals and scholars" only to highlight that they are black so they cannot be dismissed because some think they are white. They are, in every sense, intellectuals and scholars at the highest level of all ethnicities and races.

2. On June 15, 2020, in Norman, Oklahoma, the city council voted to defund the police department by $885,000.00. I made these arguments in an attempt to dissuade my ward representative from supporting decreasing the budget of the Norman Police Department.

Appendix 2

Resolution 9 That Passed in SBC's 2019 Annual Convention

On Critical Race Theory and Intersectionality

Birmingham, Alabama 2019

WHEREAS, Concerns have been raised by some evangelicals over the use of frameworks such as critical race theory and intersectionality; and

WHEREAS, Critical race theory is a set of analytical tools that explain how race has and continues to function in society, and intersectionality is the study of how different personal characteristics overlap and inform one's experience; and

WHEREAS, Critical race theory and intersectionality have been appropriated by individuals with worldviews that are contrary to the Christian faith, resulting in ideologies and methods that contradict Scripture; and

WHEREAS, Evangelical scholars who affirm the authority and sufficiency of Scripture have employed selective insights from critical race theory and intersectionality to understand multifaceted social dynamics; and

WHEREAS, The Baptist Faith and Message states, "[A]ll Scripture is totally true and trustworthy. It reveals the principles by which God judges us, and therefore is, and will remain to the end of the world, the true center of Christian union, and the supreme standard by which all human conduct, creeds, and religious opinions should be tried" (Article I); and

Appendix 2

WHEREAS, General revelation accounts for truthful insights found in human ideas that do not explicitly emerge from Scripture and reflects what some may term "common grace"; and

WHEREAS, Critical race theory and intersectionality alone are insufficient to diagnose and redress the root causes of the social ills that they identify, which result from sin, yet these analytical tools can aid in evaluating a variety of human experiences; and

WHEREAS, Scripture contains categories and principles by which to deal with racism, poverty, sexism, injustice, and abuse that are not rooted in secular ideologies; and

WHEREAS, Humanity is primarily identified in Scripture as image bearers of God, even as biblical authors address various audiences according to characteristics such as male and female, Jew and Gentile, slave and free; and

WHEREAS, The New Covenant further unites image bearers by creating a new humanity that will one day inhabit the new creation, and that the people of this new humanity, though descended from every nation, tribe, tongue, and people, are all one through the gospel of Jesus Christ (Eph 2:16; Rev 21:1–4, 9–14); and

WHEREAS, Christian citizenship is not based on our differences but instead on our common salvation in Christ—the source of our truest and ultimate identity; and

WHEREAS, The Southern Baptist Convention is committed to racial reconciliation built upon biblical presuppositions and is committed to seeking biblical justice through biblical means; now, therefore, be it

RESOLVED, That the messengers to the Southern Baptist Convention meeting in Birmingham, Alabama, June 11–12, 2019, affirm Scripture as the first, last, and sufficient authority with regard to how the Church seeks to redress social ills, and we reject any conduct, creeds, and religious opinions which contradict Scripture; and be it further

RESOLVED, That critical race theory and intersectionality should only be employed as analytical tools subordinate to Scripture—not as transcendent ideological frameworks; and be it further

RESOLVED, That the gospel of Jesus Christ alone grants the power to change people and society because "he who started a good work in you will carry it on to completion until the day of Christ Jesus" (Phil 1:6); and be it further

RESOLVED, That Southern Baptists will carefully analyze how the information gleaned from these tools are employed to address social dynamics; and be it further

RESOLVED, That Southern Baptist churches and institutions repudiate the misuse of insights gained from critical race theory, intersectionality, and any unbiblical ideologies that can emerge from their use when absolutized as a worldview; and be it further

RESOLVED, That we deny any philosophy or theology that fundamentally defines individuals using categories identified as sinful in Scripture rather than the transcendent reality shared by every image bearer and divinely affirmed distinctions; and be it further

RESOLVED, That while we denounce the misuse of critical race theory and intersectionality, we do not deny that ethnic, gender, and cultural distinctions exist and are a gift from God that will give Him absolute glory when all humanity gathers around His throne in worship because of the redemption accomplished by our resurrected Lord; and be it finally

RESOLVED, That Southern Baptist churches seek to exhibit this eschatological promise in our churches in the present by focusing on unity in Christ amid image bearers and rightly celebrate our differences as determined by God in the new creation.

Appendix 3

Resolution 9 That Passed in
SBC's 2019 Annual Convention

With My Comments

THE 2019 SBC ANNUAL meeting met on June 11–12. The messengers adopted several resolutions, one of which was a resolution on critical race theory and intersectionality.[1] While I appreciate the Resolutions Committee seeking to speak to current issues from a biblical perspective, I think this resolution lacked due consideration.

Before I suggest some nuances for the adopted resolution that I believe should have been incorporated before even considering such a resolution, I must say that I think the resolution as a whole was misdirected. To wit, if the Resolutions Committee were going to offer a resolution on critical race theory/intersectionality, their time and effort would have been better spent in precisely defining and delineating the origin and nature of critical race theory/intersectionality and why it is unnecessary and harmful to the gospel. They could have accomplished this by presenting the original Resolution 9, as written by Stephen Michael Feinstein.[2] But the committee voted no on his Resolution 9, which condemned supporting critical race theory or intersectionality and wrote a new Resolution 9 in support of them with a few caveats.

---

1. "On Critical Race Theory And Intersectionality."
2. See Appendix 4.

The Resolution, as it stands, seems to make a *seriously flawed assumption* that the messengers were sufficiently familiar with the origin, nature, and transcendent qualities of these concepts, philosophies, and their potential consequences; I would also suggest that most messengers did not fully understand them definitionally. Popular familiarity with terms should never be equated with an adequate understanding of them, particularly when voting on a resolution with such significant and far-reaching implications.

While the adopted Resolution seeks to emphasize the superiority of Scripture, it does so to stress the usability and positives of critical race theory/intersectionality so they may be adopted and employed alongside Scripture, albeit subserviently. The Resolution as adopted leaves ample room for those who either believe in these as worldviews or, at least, believe these ideological theories should be adopted as significantly useful or even essential tools for understanding and addressing human identity issues. Those of us who participated in the Conservative Resurgence have witnessed moderates undermine Scripture with better-worded documents than this Resolution. Here are the definitions of critical race theory and intersectionality.

Critical race theory is "the view that race, instead of being biologically grounded and natural, is socially constructed and that race, as a socially constructed concept, functions as a means to maintain the interests of the white population that constructed it."[3]

Intersectionality is defined in the Oxford Dictionary as "the interconnected nature of social categorizations such as race, class, and gender as they apply to a given individual or group, regarded as creating overlapping and interdependent systems of discrimination or disadvantage."[4] Consequently, minorities can suffer from varying degrees of discrimination, thereby giving them more authority to speak on race with each level.

Intersectionality is significantly related to identity politics. For example, a woman could suffer discrimination, but a black woman suffers two compounding levels of discrimination. If the black woman is a lesbian, then she suffers on three levels. Thus, a person's identity is wrapped up in the degree to which they are discriminated. The more layers of discrimination generally include how much authority we should grant their opinions. Of course, the white man suffers from no levels of discrimination.

3. Curry, "Critical Race Theory."
4. "Intersectionality."

An example of the stronger and clearer wording that I think is missing from the Resolution can be found in *The Statement on Social Justice & The Gospel*. The first affirmation and disaffirmation state:

> WE AFFIRM that the Bible is God's Word, breathed out by him. It is inerrant, infallible, and the final authority for determining what is true (what we must believe) and what is right (how we must live). All truth claims and ethical standards must be tested by God's final Word, which is Scripture alone.

> WE DENY that Christian belief, character, or conduct can be dictated by any other authority, and we deny that the postmodern ideologies derived from intersectionality, radical feminism, and critical race theory are consistent with biblical teaching. We further deny that competency to teach on any biblical issue comes from any qualification for spiritual people other than clear understanding and simple communication of what is revealed in Scripture.[5]

Following is the Resolution as adopted. I have inserted some suggestions that I think should have been incorporated before even considering the Resolution as worthy of debate. My suggestions strongly indicate that *at least some* of the authors of the Resolution granted more credibility to critical race theory/intersectionality than is necessary or even biblically prudent. My suggestions are italicized and in brackets; my comments are not intended to reflect the grammatical changes necessary for proper wording but only the ideas.

Resolution 9, As Adopted, On Critical Race Theory and Intersectionality

WHEREAS, Concerns have been raised by some evangelicals over the use of frameworks such as critical race theory and intersectionality; and

WHEREAS, Critical race theory is a set of analytical tools [*and philosophy*] that [*seeks to*] explain how race has and continues to function in society, and intersectionality is the [*replace "the" with "a"*] study of how different personal characteristics overlap and [*attempt to*] inform one's experience; and

WHEREAS, Critical race theory and intersectionality [*originated as contradictory to the Christian faith and*] have been appropriated by individuals

5. https://statementonsocialjustice.com/.

with worldviews that are contrary to the Christian faith, resulting in ideologies and methods that contradict Scripture; and

WHEREAS, Evangelical scholars [*insert "Some" before Evangelical—note the favoritism of the drafters in that they used "some evangelicals" have concerns about using critical race theory/intersectionality in the first Whereas but left it out in this Whereas that speaks of employment of these concepts by evangelicals—subtle*] who affirm the authority and sufficiency of Scripture [*which is the precise designation that many moderates, who deny inerrancy, used prior to and during the Conservative Resurgence in the SBC, and therefore, is inadequate for this kind of resolution; it omits words like "inerrancy" or "verbal plenary inspiration"*] have employed selective insights from critical race theory and intersectionality to understand multifaceted social dynamics; and

WHEREAS, The Baptist Faith and Message states, "All Scripture is totally true and trustworthy. It reveals the principles by which God judges us, and therefore is, and will remain to the end of the world, the true center of Christian union, and the supreme standard by which all human conduct, creeds, and religious opinions should be tried" (Article I); and

WHEREAS, General revelation accounts for truthful insights found in human ideas that do not explicitly emerge from Scripture and reflects what some may term "common grace"; and

WHEREAS, Critical race theory and intersectionality alone are insufficient [*replace "insufficient" with "incapable"*] to diagnose and redress the root causes of the social ills that they [*claim to*] identify, which result from sin, yet these analytical [*philosophical ideas and*] tools can [*replace "can" with "may"*] aid in evaluating a variety of human experiences; and

WHEREAS, Scripture contains categories and principles by which to deal with racism, poverty, sexism, injustice, and abuse that are not rooted in secular ideologies; and

WHEREAS, Humanity is primarily identified in Scripture as image bearers of God, even as biblical authors address various audiences according to characteristics such as male and female, Jew and Gentile, slave and free; and

WHEREAS, The New Covenant further unites image bearers by creating a new humanity that will one day inhabit the new creation, and that the people of this new humanity, though descended from every nation, tribe, tongue, and people, are all one through the gospel of Jesus Christ (Eph 2:16; Rev 21:1–4, 9–14); and

WHEREAS, Christian citizenship is not based on our differences but instead on our common salvation in Christ—the source of our truest and ultimate identity; and

WHEREAS, The Southern Baptist Convention is committed to racial reconciliation built upon biblical presuppositions and is committed to seeking biblical justice through biblical means; now, therefore, be it

RESOLVED, That the messengers to the Southern Baptist Convention meeting in Birmingham, Alabama, June 11–12, 2019, affirm Scripture as the first, last, and sufficient authority with regard to how the Church seeks to redress social ills, and we reject any conduct, creeds, and religious opinions which contradict Scripture [*or marginalizes or distracts from the cure for people's identity problems being found in Christ alone*]; and be it further

RESOLVED, That critical race theory and intersectionality should only be employed as analytical tools [*replace "tools" with "considerations"*] subordinate to Scripture—not as transcendent ideological frameworks [*as many secularists who use them believe*]; and be it further

RESOLVED, That the gospel of Jesus Christ alone grants the power to change people and society because "he who started a good work in you will carry it on to completion until the day of Christ Jesus" (Phil 1:6); and be it further

RESOLVED, That Southern Baptists will carefully analyze how the information gleaned from these tools are employed to address social dynamics; and be it further

RESOLVED, That Southern Baptist churches and institutions repudiate the misuse [*the preceding wording of the Resolution is imprecise enough to guarantee disagreement as to what constitutes "misuse"*] of insights gained from critical race theory, intersectionality, and any unbiblical ideologies that can emerge from their use when absolutized as a worldview [*or even used as an indispensably important analytical tool*]; and be it further

RESOLVED, That we deny any philosophy or theology that fundamentally defines individuals using categories identified as sinful in Scripture rather than the transcendent reality shared by every image bearer and divinely affirmed distinctions; and be it further

RESOLVED, That while we denounce the misuse of critical race theory and intersectionality, we do not deny that ethnic, gender, and cultural distinctions exist and are a gift from God that will give Him absolute glory when all humanity gathers around His throne in worship because of the redemption accomplished by our resurrected Lord; and be it finally

RESOLVED, That Southern Baptist churches seek to exhibit this eschatological promise in our churches in the present by focusing on unity in Christ amid image bearers and rightly celebrate our differences as determined by God in the new creation.

Appendix 4

Original Resolution 9 That Was
Rejected by the Resolution Committee

SBC19 Resolution #9 on
Critical Race Theory and Intersectionality

by Stephen Feinstein

AT THIS TIME YESTERDAY, passions heated up at the Southern Baptist Annual Convention. The resolutions committee presented the messengers with Resolution #9, which ended up in a heated, yet short, debate. Presently, there is a lot of noise on social media over this. Many are speaking on this issue, and necessity lays the same mandate upon me.

Why should my voice be included? Simply put, I am the one who authored the resolution. My name is Stephen Feinstein, a graduate of Southern Baptist Theological Seminary, a pastor of Sovereign Way Christian Church in Hesperia, CA, and a Chaplain (MAJ) in the United States Army Reserves. Like many, I am alarmed at the proliferation of toxic, divisive, and satanic rhetoric designed to divide humanity and facilitate constant opposition in our society. Even worse, it has seeped into Bible colleges and some seminaries. I have had parents come to me for advice when their child came home from a conservative Bible college complaining about white privilege. I was present at the Shepherds Conference when my favorite evangelical leaders appeared to be divided on how to handle this issue.

Therefore, I determined after the Shepherds Conference that I would propose a resolution denouncing critical race theory and intersectionality.

Well, on Wednesday morning, June 12, 2019, the messengers were given copies of the resolutions. Although I was stoked that my resolution was accepted, I also immediately noticed the committee severely altered what I had submitted. It is their right to do so. I have been asked to make public the resolution as I submitted it, and so I will do so here. I will not comment on it here, but simply post it. I plan on making a short video sharing my thoughts on the resolution as it now stands. I pray you will be gracious and patient with me. I had to set aside my blog four years ago due to a high workload. I have been wanting to jump back into it, and it seems that this issue is the catalyst. See the original resolution below.

Resolution Author: Stephen Feinstein
Sovereign Way Christian Church
Pastor(s): Stephen Feinstein; Brian Orr; Joshua Ritchie
Stephen Feinstein
pastorsteve@sovereignway.org

Sovereign Way Christian Church
15660 Juniper Street
Hesperia, CA 92345
760-948-3200
info@sovereignway.org
Website:https://sovereignway.org/

On Critical Race Theory and Intersectionality

WHEREAS, all Scripture is totally true and trustworthy and reveals the principles by which God judges us, and therefore is, and will remain to the end of the world, the true center of Christian union, and the supreme standard by which all human conduct, creeds, and religious opinions should be tried; and

WHEREAS, critical race theory and intersectionality are founded upon un-biblical presuppositions descended from Marxist theories and categories, and therefore are inherently opposed to the Scriptures as the true center of Christian union; and

Appendix 4

WHEREAS, both critical race theory and intersectionality as ideologies have infiltrated some Southern Baptist churches and institutions—institutions funded by the Cooperative Program; and

WHEREAS, critical race theory upholds postmodern relativistic understandings of truth; and

WHEREAS, critical race theory divides humanity into groups of oppressors and oppressed, and is used to encourage biblical, transcendental truth claims to be considered suspect when communicated from groups labeled as oppressors; and

WHEREAS, intersectionality defines human identity by race, social background, gender, sexual orientation, religion, and a host of other distinctions, and it does so at the expense of other identities; and

WHEREAS, intersectionality reduces human beings to distinguishable identities of unequal value and thus reduces human identity down to differences rather than commonality; and

WHEREAS, intersectionality encourages rage as its driving energy and conclusion; and

WHEREAS, intersectionality magnifies differences while deeming as more favorable the individuals who combine the highest number of oppressed identities; and

WHEREAS, both critical race theory and intersectionality breed division and deny humanity's essential commonality; and

WHEREAS, the Scripture provides God's narrative on such matters; and

WHEREAS, the book of Genesis grounds humanity in that which unites us, namely our common identity as the Imago Dei, which itself is the foundation of every biblical, ethical command to love one's neighbor and to seek justice for all; and

WHEREAS, the Bible acknowledges differences—male and female, slave and free, Jew and Gentile—it does not begin with human differences, but instead begins with what unites humanity, namely the Imago Dei; and

WHEREAS, the sameness of humanity built upon the Imago Dei, justifies the value of all individuals in something that transcends race, gender, and other identity intersections; and

WHEREAS, the New Covenant further unites by creating a new humanity that will one day inhabit the new heavens and the new earth, and that the people of this new humanity, though descended from every nation, tribe, tongue, and people, are all one in Christ; and

WHEREAS, this new humanity is comprised of people from every ethnicity and race, of every socio-economic background and culture, and yet these people enter this new humanity through belief in the Gospel of Jesus Christ; and

WHEREAS, Christian citizenship is not based on our differences but instead on our common salvation in Christ; and

WHEREAS, we find our true identity in Christ; and

WHEREAS, the Scriptures have categories and principles by which to deal with racism, sexism, injustice, abuse—principles found in prior Southern Baptist resolutions such as "On the Anti-Gospel of Alt-Right White Supremacy," for example, that are not rooted in Marxist anti-gospel presuppositions; and

WHEREAS, the rhetoric of critical race theory and intersectionality found in some Southern Baptist institutions and leaders is causing unnecessary and unbiblical division among the body of Christ and is tarnishing the reputation of the Southern Baptist Convention as a whole, inviting charges of theological liberalism, egalitarianism, and Marxism; and

WHEREAS, the Southern Baptist Convention is committed to racial reconciliation built upon biblical presuppositions, and is committed to seeking biblical justice through biblical means; now, therefore, be it

RESOLVED, That the messengers to the Southern Baptist Convention, meeting in Birmingham, Alabama, June 11–12, 2019, decry every philosophy or theology, including critical race theory and intersectionality, as antithetical to the Gospel of Jesus Christ, since they divide the people of Christ by defining fundamental identity as something other than our identity in Jesus Christ; and be it further

RESOLVED, That we deny any philosophy or theology that defines individuals primarily by non-transcendental social constructs rather than by the transcendental reality of all humans existing as the Imago Dei; and be it further

RESOLVED, That while we denounce critical race theory and intersectionality, we do not deny that ethnic, gender, cultural, and racial distinctions do in fact exist and are a gift from God that will give Him absolute glory when the entire gamut of human diversity worships Him in perfect unity founded upon our unity in Jesus Christ; and be it further

RESOLVED, That Southern Baptist Churches will seek to paint this eschatological picture in a proleptic manner in our churches in the present by focusing on our unity in Christ and our common humanity as the Imago Dei rather than dividing over the secondary matters than make us different; and be it further

RESOLVED, That Southern Baptists Churches and institutions will take a prophetic stand against all forms of biblically-defined injustice, but we will do so in a manner consistent with the biblical worldview rather than unbiblical worldviews; and be it further

RESOLVED, That Southern Baptist institutions need to make progress in rooting out the intentional promulgation of critical race theory and intersectionality in both our churches and institutions; and be it further

RESOLVED, That we earnestly pray, both for those who advocate ideologies meant to divide believers along intersectional lines and those who are thereby deceived, that they may see their error through the light of the Gospel, repent of these anti-Gospel beliefs, and come to know the peace and love of Christ through redeemed fellowship in the Kingdom of God, which is established from every nation, tribe, people, and language.

Appendix 5

Some Helpful Links

1. "By What Standard? God's World . . . God's Rules" at https://founders. org/cinedoc/ provides an overview of some troubling tendencies and trends in the SBC.

2. Enemieswithinthechurch.com provides several articles on cultural Marxism problems in evangelicalism and is producing a movie about social justice and white privilege. The trailer and articles are well worth reading and watching.

3. Jon Harris deals with several issues, which allow you to hear people in their own words such as woke professors at Southeastern Baptist Theological Seminary and others. http://www.worldviewconversation.com/

4. Dr. E. S. Williams, a member of Charles Spurgeon's London Metropolitan Tabernacle Church, explains critical race theory and intersectionality and presents his case for Albert Mohler's significant involvement in spreading them in the SBC. https://www.youtube. com/watch?v=MIlnLU-vt_g&feature=youtu.be

5. Here is a superb article by B. Nathaniel Sullivan on Resolution 9. https://www.wordfoundations.com/an-excerpt-from-two-underlying-things-about-of-resolution-9-that-are-affronts-to-scripture-despite-the-resolutions-declarations-to-the-contrary/

Authorial Glossary

Biblical Justice

This type of justice emanates from God's holy, impartial, and loving nature (Lev 19:2; Acts 10:34; 1 John 4:8). Everyone is created in the image of God (Gen 1:26–27). They are, therefore, equal by nature and under the same righteous standard of justice, which equality should prevail in societies as well.[1] Everyone has sinned against God and falls short of his holy and just standard (Rom 3:10). Each person is accountable for only his sin (Ezek 18:19–21, 32; 33:11). Because God is love (1 John 4:8, 16), he desires to save every person from their due judgment for their sin, and he has provisioned so that everyone can be saved (John 1:29; 3:16; 20:30–31). In Christ, all barriers are broken down (Gal 3:28; Eph 2:14–15; Col 1:20). All who are in Christ are to carry the gospel of reconciliation to the world (Rom 5:10; 2 Cor 5:18–21) and to reflect God's impartial and unifying justice toward everyone (Exod 23:3; Lev 19:15; Mic 6:8), compassionately ministering to the genuinely needy (Deut 10:18; Ps 140:12; Ezek 22:29; 1 Tim 5:3; Jas 1:27).

Conservative Baptist Network (CBN)

"The Conservative Baptist Network is a partnership of Southern Baptists where all generations are encouraged, equipped, and empowered to bring positive, biblical solutions that strengthen the SBC in an effort to fulfill the Great Commission and influence culture."
https://conservativebaptistnetwork.com/

---

1. The other word signifying essential equality is ontologically equal.

Critical Race Theory

"Race instead of being biologically grounded and natural is socially constructed; and that race as a socially constructed concept functions as a means to maintain the interests of the white population that constructed it."[2] The concept of race serves as a mechanism for white people to promote pervasive institutional racism in order to maintain white supremacy.[3] Critical race theory makes racism (white supremacy and privilege) present in *every* interracial interaction and relationship. Therefore, the question, according to critical race theory, is not is racism present, but instead, the question is, how is racism present in this situation. Critical race theory is a part of cultural Marxism. Cultural Marxism is composed of a broad set of ideas that serve as instruments for a societal transformation to bring about the redistribution of power and wealth.[4] For example, white people need to repent of white supremacy and privilege, but black people do not need to repent. Even if a white person has never had a genuinely racist thought or he has repented of past racism, he is still a racist because he is of the white majority.[5]

Critical Theory

It focuses on culture in order to change it in contrast to other social theories that focus on understanding society. It presupposes some people are oppressed and in need of deliverance.

Intersectionality

This term encompasses interconnected social categories such as race, sex, and sexual orientation, which can serve as components of multi-layered discrimination and oppression.[6] For example, as a minority, a woman could suffer discrimination, but a black woman suffers two compounding levels

2. Curry, "Critical Race Theory."

3. Both critical race theory and cultural Marxism are a part of critical theory.

4. Cultural Marxism is the application of Marxist concepts to marginalized groups rather than classes as in classical Marxism. For further definition of critical race theory see, https://www.britannica.com/topic/critical-race-theory.

5. True racism is the belief that one's own race is inherently superior to another, and others being inherently inferior, cannot overcome their inferiority.

6. See also https://www.lexico.com/en/definition/intersectionality.

of discrimination. If the black woman is a lesbian, she then suffers on three levels. A person's identity and authority are wrapped up in the degree to which the person suffers discrimination (the basis of identity politics). In cultural Marxism, of which intersectionality is a part, truth claims made by the oppressors are always suspect. In contrast, truth claims made by the oppressed are always credible until proven wrong, which intersectionality makes almost impossible. Think about how accusations of abuse in the Me-Too movement are accepted as truth without evidence, while the accused is assumed to be lying—guilty until proven innocent.

Social Justice

This term is generally interchangeable with cultural Marxism. This type of justice is accomplished by favoring one group (the oppressed/minority/non-sinners) and punishing the other group (the oppressors/majority/sinners) by redistribution of wealth, power, and privilege. Redistribution can be accomplished by civil measures or revolution and forced redistribution of wealth and power.[7] As in Marxism, social justice emphasizes group identity and responsibility rather than individual identity and responsibility. The groups may be composed of people who neither suffered nor inflicted wrong. Merit or guilt is based on such things as skin color or sex. Social justice determines what is wrong or right, and what the penalties or corrections should be. These may be antithetical to true biblical justice. Social justice's identity politics divide rather than unite.

Southern Baptist Convention (SBC)

As a convention of churches, our missional vision is to present the gospel of Jesus Christ to every person in the world and to make disciples of all the nations.

7. The Encyclopedia Britannica says, "Critical theory: Marxist-inspired movement in social and political philosophy originally associated with the work of the Frankfurt School. Drawing particularly on the thought of Karl Marx and Sigmund Freud, critical theorists maintain that a primary goal of the philosophy is to understand and to help overcome the social structures through which people are dominated and oppressed." See "Critical Theory."

It is important to keep in mind that Marx, Friedrich Engels, and Sigmund Freud were all materialists. They denied God, the soul and spirit of man, and the entire immaterial world, which makes them absolutely in opposition to Christianity.

Systemic

Systemic is also called structural. It is the idea that the systems and structures of America disadvantage black people. It is the means by which white people (white supremacists) maintain their advantage. The evidence of systemic racism is reliant on various success indicators. The emphasis on systemic racism affords little or no consideration of how other non-racial factors may affect the success of blacks or people of color. If a person contends that racism alone can be systemic or that unequal outcomes always indicate injustice, he is speaking as a Marxist. Systemic racism should not be accepted as a given, even though that is a prevalent sentiment. Those who claim the impediment to black people's ability to advance is due to systemic racism must prove that to be the case. Proof requires more than relying on how things were in the past or anecdotal racism.

Bibliography

Ascol, Tom. "By What Standard? God's World . . . God's Rules." https://founders.org/cinedoc/.

Angst, Maggie. "On Fourth Day of Protests, Newsom Tells Demonstrators: 'Your Rage Is Real. Express It.'" *Santa Cruz Sentinel*, June 1, 2020. https://www.santacruzsentinel.com/2020/06/01/trump-tells-governors-to-dominate-protesters-newsom-tells-them-you-matter-i-care/.

Baptist Press Staff. "Southern Baptist Leaders Issue Joint Statement on the Death of George Floyd." *Baptist Press*, May 30, 2020. http://bpnews.net/54877/southern-baptist-leaders-issue-joint-statement-on-the-death-of-george-floyd.

Barbieri, Louis A., Jr. "Matthew." In *The Bible Knowledge Commentary: An Exposition of the Scriptures*, edited by J. F. Walvoord and R. B. Zuck, 2:18–94. Wheaton, IL: Victor Books, 1985. Logos electronic edition.

Baucham, Voddie. "Irreconcilable Views of Reconciliation." https://www.gty.org/library/sermons-library/TM19-9/irreconcilable-views-of-reconciliation-voddie-baucham.

Berlin, Ira. *Slaves without Masters: The Free Negro in the Antebellum South*. New York: Pantheon, 1974.

Berry, Daina Ramey. "American Slavery: Separating Fact from Fiction." *The Conversation*, June 19, 2017. https://theconversation.com/american-slavery-separating-fact-from-myth-79620.

Biden, Joe. "Let Me Be Very Clear." *Twitter*, March 24, 2020. https://twitter.com/JoeBiden/status/1242604610319192065.

Bohman, James. "Critical Theory." *Stanford Encyclopedia of Philosophy*, March 8, 2005. Edited by Edward N. Zalta. https://plato.stanford.edu/archives/win2019/entries/critical-theory/.

Bozeman, William P., et al. "Injuries Associated with Police Use of Force." *Journal of Trauma and Acute Care Surgery* 84.3 (2018) 466–72. doi: 10.1097/TA.0000000000001783.

Briggs, Megan. "This Is Why Al Mohler Didn't Sign the Statement on Social Justice." *ChurchLeaders.com*. 10/1/18. https://churchleaders.com/news/334586-al-mohler-sign-statement-on-social-justice.html.

Burton, Tara Isabella. "The March for Life, America's Biggest Anti-abortion Rally, Explained." *Vox*, January 18, 2018. https://www.vox.com/identities/2018/1/18/16870018/march-for-life-anti-abortion-rally-explained.

Byron. "Thomas Sowell: Marx the Man." *YouTube*, August 3, 2018. https://m.youtube.com/watch?v=heGapg-08yE.

Bibliography

Campbell, Donald K. "Galatians." In *The Bible Knowledge Commentary: An Exposition of the Scriptures,* edited by J. F. Walvoord and R. B. Zuck, 2:587–612. Wheaton, IL: Victor, 1985. Logos electronic edition.

Chafer, Lewis Sperry. *Systematic Theology.* 8 vols. Dallas: Dallas Seminary Press, 1948.

Chamberlain, Samuel. "Riots Break Out Across America after George Floyd Death." *Fox News,* May 29, 2020. https://www.foxnews.com/us/live-updates-riots-break-out-across-america-after-george-floyd-death.

Chandler, Diana. "Pastors Urge Prayer, Gospel Outreach as Outrage Grows Over George Floyd's Death." *Baptist Press,* May 27, 2020. http://www.bpnews.net/54859/pastors-urge-prayer-gospel-outreach-as-outrage-grows-over-george-floyds-death.

Cone, James H. *Black Theology and Black Power.* New York: Seabury, 1969.

———. *A Black Theology of Liberation.* Philadelphia: Lippencott, 1970.

Conservative Baptist Network. "Statement Regarding George Floyd and the Ensuing Riots." May 30, 2020. https://conservativebaptistnetwork.com/statement-regarding-george-floyd-and-the-ensuing-riots/.

"Critical Theory." https://www.britannica.com/topic/critical-theory.

Curry, Tommy. "Critical Race Theory." *Encyclopædia Britannica.* https://www.britannica.com/topic/critical-race-theory.

"#DefundThePolice." https://blacklivesmatter.com/defundthepolice/.

DiAngelo, Robin D. "Anti-Racism Handout." https://robindiangelo.com/wp-content/uploads/2016/06/Anti-racism-handout-1-page-2016.pdf.

Elisabeth, Léo. "The French Antilles." In *Neither Slave Nor Free: The Freedman of African Descent in the Slave Societies of the New World,* edited by David W. Cohen and Jack P. Greene, 134–71. Baltimore: Johns Hopkins University Press, 1972.

"Fast Facts about the SBC." https://web.archive.org/web/20200619171521/http://www.sbc.net/BecomingSouthernBaptist/FastFacts.asp.

Feinstein, Stephen. "SBC19 Resolution #9 on Critical Race Theory and Intersectionality." *SovereignWay* (blog), June 13, 2019. https://sovereignway.blogspot.com/2019/06/sbc19-resolution-9-on-critical-race.html?m=1.

Felder, Ben. "Norman Council Reduces Police Budget as Cities Confront Calls to Cut PD Spending." *The Frontier,* June 17, 2020. https://www.readfrontier.org/stories/norman-council-reduces-police-budget-as-cities-confront-calls-to-cut-pd-spending/.

For the New Christian Intellectual. "'I Am a Racist'—Matthew Hall, Provost at Southern Seminary." *YouTube,* July 31, 2019. https://www.youtube.com/watch?v=1IiKCYSevDU.

Founders Ministries. "Racial Reconciliation—Ephesians 2:10–11 | Dr. Voddie Baucham." *YouTube,* March 27, 2019. https://www.youtube.com/watch?v=FoJGYCc7EUg.

Freedom Forum. "Martha MacCallum Interviews BLM Leader Hawk Newsom 6/25/2020." *YouTube,* June 25, 2020. https://www.youtube.com/watch?v=5ClaPgXpOag.

Gardner, Llew. "TV Interview for Thames TV This Week." *Thames Television,* February 5, 1976. https://www.margaretthatcher.org/document/102953.

Garrett, James Leo, Jr. *Systematic Theology: Biblical, Historical, and Evangelical.* 2 vols. Eugene, OR: Wipf & Stock, 1990.

Gatewood, Willard B. *Aristocrats of Color: The Black Elite, 1880–1920.* Bloomington: Indiana University Press, 1990.

Geisler, Norman. *Systematic Theology.* 4 vols. Bloomington, MN: Bethany, 2004.

"Genocide: Black Abortions in America." https://www.grrtl.org/genocide/.

Bibliography

Genovese, Eugene D. "The Slave States of North America." In *Neither Slave nor Free: The Freedman of African Descent in the Slave Societies of the New World,* edited by David W. Cohen and Jack P. Greene, 258–77. Baltimore: Johns Hopkins University Press, 1972.

Gorkin, Katharine. "How the 1960s Riots Foreshadow Today's Communist Weaponization of Black Pain." *The Federalist,* September 14, 2020. https://thefederalist.com/2020/09/14/how-the-1960s-riots-foreshadow-todays-communist-weaponization-of-black-pain/.

Grabmeier, Jeff. "When Europeans Were Slaves: Research Suggests White Slavery Was Much More Common Than Previously Believed." *Ohio State News,* March 7, 2004. https://news.osu.edu/when-europeans-were-slaves--research-suggests-white-slavery-was-much-more-common-than-previously-believed/.

Gray, Lewis Cecil. *History of Agriculture in the Southern United States to 1860, vol 1.* Glouster, MS: Smith, 1958.

"Great Society." https://www.history.com/topics/1960s/great-society.

Hall, Matthew J. "'For He Is Our Peace': The Centrality of the Gospel of Christ in Racial Reconciliation." *Southern Equip,* November 26, 2019. https://equip.sbts.edu/article/peace-centrality-gospel-christ-racial-reconciliation/.

Handler, Jerome S., and Arnold A. Sio. "Barbados." In *Neither Slave nor Free: The Freedman of African Descent in the Slave Societies of the New World,* edited by David W. Cohen and Jack P. Greene, 214–57. Baltimore: Johns Hopkins University Press, 1972.

Hoover Institution. "Discrimination and Disparities with Thomas Sowell." *YouTube,* May 3, 2018. https://www.youtube.com/watch?v=U7hmTRT8tb4.

———. "Thomas Sowell Is Back Again to Discuss His Book Wealth, Poverty, and Politics." *YouTube,* September 27, 2016. https://www.youtube.com/watch?v=ICsPQnGJEpY.

———. "Thomas Sowell on the Myths of Economic Inequality." *YouTube,* December 3, 2018. https://www.youtube.com/watch?v=mS5WYp5xmvI.

———. "Thomas Sowell Talks about His New Book Economic Facts and Fallacies." *YouTube,* September 26, 2008. https://www.youtube.com/watch?v=noMaY33LJZo.

———. "Wealth, Poverty, and Politics." *YouTube,* December 8, 2015. https://www.youtube.com/watch?v=sGYl17DiEwo.

"Intersectionality." https://www.lexico.com/en/definition/intersectionality.

John, Joseph R. "Black Lives Matter Co-Founder Confirms that Violent Mob Movement Is Run by 'Trained Marxists.'" *Citizens Journal,* July 22, 2020. https://www.citizensjournal.us/black-lives-matter-co-founder-confirms-that-violent-mob-movement-is-run-by-trained-marxists/.

Kaczynski, Andrew. "Joe Biden Described Being an 'Odd Man Out' with Democrats on Abortion in 2006 Interview." *CNN,* June 13, 2019. https://www.cnn.com/2019/06/13/politics/joe-biden-abortion/index.html.

Kim, Anthony B., and Julia Howe. *Why Democratic Socialists Can't Legitimately Claim Sweden or Denmark as Success Stories.* Washington, DC: The Heritage Foundation, 2018.

King, Martin Luther, Jr. "I Have a Dream." https://www.americanrhetoric.com/speeches/mlkihaveadream.htm.

Kirschner, Stephen Thomas. "Cultural Marxism: The Origins of the Present Day Social Justice Movement, and Political Correctness." *The Policy,* February 14, 2017. https://thepolicy.us/cultural-marxism-the-origins-of-the-present-day-social-justice-movement-and-political-correctness-ffb89c6ef4f1.

Bibliography

Koger, Larry. *Black Slaveowners: Free Black Masters in South Carolina, 1790–1860*. Columbia, SC: University of South Carolina Press, 1995.

Koseff, Alexi. "Newsom Signs Bill to Fix Sex Offender Registry Law that Penalized Gay People." *San Francisco Chronicle*, September 11, 2020. https://www.sfchronicle.com/politics/article/Newsom-signs-bill-to-fix-sex-offender-registry-15561586.php.

Levin, Mark. "Bob Woodson Joins Mark Levin on 'Life, Liberty & Levin.'" *Fox News*, March 6, 2020. https://video.foxnews.com/v/6138889433001#sp=show-clips.

———. "Thomas Sowell Discusses 'Systemic Racism' Claims with 'Life, Liberty & Levin.'" *Fox News*, July 10, 2020. https://video.foxnews.com/v/6170820682001#sp=show-clips.

———. "Thomas Sowell on 'Utter Madness' of Defund the Police Push, Wonders Whether the US Is Reaching Point of No Return." *Fox News*, July 12, 2020. foxnews.com/transcript/thomas-sowell-on-utter-madness-of-defund-the-police-push-wonders-whether-us-is-reaching-point-of-no-return.

Lincoln, Abraham. "The Gettysburg Address." http://www.abrahamlincolnonline.org/lincoln/speeches/gettysburg.htm.

Lindsay, James. "For Racial Healing, Reject Critical Race Theory." *Roca News*, September 4, 2020. https://www.rocanews.com/blog-posts/for-racial-healing-reject-critical-race-theory.

Mac Donald, Heather. *The Diversity Delusion: How Race and Gender Pandering Corrupt the University and Undermine Our Culture*. New York: St. Martin's Griffin, 2018.

Martin, Rod D. "With Great Respect." *Twitter*, February 15, 2020. https://twitter.com/RodDMartin/status/1228725942627033088.

Marx, Karl, and Friedrich Engels. "Chapter IV: Position of the Communists in Relation to the Various Existing Opposition Parties." https://www.marxists.org/archive/marx/works/1848/communist-manifesto/ch04.htm.

McKissic, Dwight. "You Would Think." *Twitter*, March 25, 2020. https://twitter.com/pastordmack/status/1242813718385373186.

Memmott, Mark. "Nellie Gray, Founder Of 'March For Life,' Dies." *NPR*, August 15, 2012. https://www.npr.org/sections/thetwo-way/2012/08/15/158820517/nellie-gray-founder-of-march-for-life-dies.

Mohler, Albert. "The Briefing." https://albertmohler.com/2019/06/14/briefing-6-14-19.

———. "The Real Network of Southern Baptists Is Called the Southern Baptist Convention." *Twitter*, February 15, 2020. https://twitter.com/albertmohler/status/1228722925412458496.

———. "Southern Baptists Are Up to the Challenge of Talking to One Another about Difficult Questions." *Twitter*, February 5, 2020. https://twitter.com/albertmohler/status/1225179246940827650.

Morgan, Philip D. "Black Life in Eighteenth-Century Charleston." *Perspectives in American History* (new series) 1 (1984) 187–232.

Murdock, Deroy. "Looting and Rioting after George Floyd Killing Drew Shocking Support from Left." *Fox News*, June 9, 2020. https://www.foxnews.com/opinion/george-floyd-democrats-police-deroy-murdock.

———. "Rioters Do Injustice to George Floyd, Tortured and Killed in a Case of Police Brutality." *Fox News*, May 29, 2020. https://www.foxnews.com/opinion/deroy-murdock-rioters-do-injustice-to-george-floyd-killed-in-a-horrific-case-of-police-brutality.

"NAACP History: W. E. B. Dubois." https://www.naacp.org/naacp-history-w-e-b-dubois/.

Nobile, Philip. "Uncovering Roots." *Village Voice*, February 23, 1993.

"On Critical Race Theory and Intersectionality." https://www.sbc.net/resource-library/resolutions/on-critical-race-theory-and-intersectionality/.

"On Sensitivity and Unity Regarding the Confederate Battle Flag." https://www.sbc.net/resource-library/resolutions/on-sensitivity-and-unity-regarding-the-confederate-battle-flag/.

"On the Anti-gospel of Alt-right White Supremacy." https://www.sbc.net/resource-library/resolutions/on-the-anti-gospel-of-alt-right-white-supremacy/.

Ordway, Denise-Marie. "Police Use of Force." *Journalist's Resource*, May 1, 2018. https://journalistsresource.org/studies/government/criminal-justice/police-use-of-force-injuries-research/.

Perlman, Merrill. "The Origin of the Term 'Intersectionality.'" *Columbia Journalism Review*, October 23, 2018. https://www.cjr.org/language_corner/intersectionality.php.

PJ Tibayan. "Albert Mohler on Social Justice and the Gospel at SBTS Chapel." *YouTube* September 14, 2018. https://www.youtube.com/watch?v=5elrmVgBddU.

Powers, Bernard E., Jr. *Black Charlestonians: A Social History, 1822–1885*. Fayetteville: University of Arkansas Press, 1994.

"Racism." https://dictionary.cambridge.org/us/dictionary/english/racism.

"Racism." https://www.merriam-webster.com/dictionary/racism.

Rankin, David C. "The Impact of the Civil War on the Free Color Community of New Orleans." *Perspectives in American History* 11 (1977–88) 377–416.

The Real News Network. "A Short History of Black Lives Matter." *YouTube* July 23, 2015. https://www.youtube.com/watch?v=Zp-RswgpjD8.

"Resolution on Racial Reconciliation on the 150th Anniversary of the Southern Baptist Convention." https://www.sbc.net/resource-library/resolutions/resolution-on-racial-reconciliation-on-the-150th-anniversary-of-the-southern-baptist-convention/.

Ring, Edward. "When Will A Prominent Black Athlete Stand Up to the Mob?" *American Greatness*, September 3, 2020. https://amgreatness.com/2020/09/03/when-will-a-prominent-black-athlete-stand-up-to-the-mob/.

Roach, David. "Social Justice Statement Spurs 'Productive Conversation.'" *Baptist Press*, September 7, 2018. https://www.baptistpress.com/resource-library/news/social-justice-statement-spurs-productive-conversation/.

Robinson, Peter. "The Case against Revolution with Ayaan Hirsi Ali." *Uncommon Knowledge*, June 30, 2020. https://www.hoover.org/research/case-against-revolution-ayaan-hirsi-ali.

Rogers, Ronnie W. *Does God Love All or Some? Comparing Biblical Extensivism and Calvinism's Exclusivism*. Eugene, OR: Wipf & Stock, 2019.

———. "In Defense of God's Order and the Gospel." Sermon series, February–April 2020. https://www.sermonaudio.com/search.asp?sourceonly=true&currSection=sermonsource&keyword=trinitynorman&subsetcat=series&subsetitem=God%27s+order+and+the+gospel.

———. "The Right and Wrong of the Houston Chronicle's Articles on 'Abuse of Faith.'" https://ronniewrogers.com/2019/02/18/the-right-and-wrong-of-the-houston-chronicles-articles-on-abuse-of-faith/.

———. "Trouble in the SBC: Some Helpful Links." https://ronniewrogers.com/2020/02/13/trouble-in-the-sbc-some-helpful-links/.

Bibliography

Rojas, Rick. "'It's Got to Stop': Atlanta's Mayor Decries a Surge of Violence as a Girl Is Killed." *New York Times*, July 6, 2020. https://www.nytimes.com/2020/07/06/us/atlanta-mayor-8-year-old-killed.html.

Rousselle, Christine. "Churches in 6 States Damaged by Violent Protests." Catholic News Agency, June 1, 2020. https://www.catholicnewsagency.com/news/cathedrals-in-6-states-damaged-by-violent-protests-91111.

Rufo, Christopher F. "Summary of Critical Race Theory Investigations." https://christopherrufo.com/summary-of-critical-race-theory-investigations/.

Schoenberg, Shira. "Healey: 'America Is Burning. But That's How Forests Grow.'" *CommonWealth Magazine*, June 2, 2020. https://commonwealthmagazine.org/criminal-justice/healey-america-is-burning-but-thats-how-forests-grow/.

Schurz, Carl, et al. *The Reminiscences of Carl Schurz*. Vol. 1, *1829–1852*. New York: Doubleday, 1909.

Siders, David. "Biden Calls for Enshrining Roe v. Wade in Federal Law." *Politico*, June 22, 2019. https://www.politico.com/story/2019/06/22/biden-roe-v-wade-2020-1376712.

Smith, Samuel. "Al Mohler Explains Why He Didn't Sign John MacArthur's Anti-social Justice Statement." *Christian Post*, March 11, 2019. https://www.christianpost.com/news/al-mohler-explains-why-he-didnt-sign-john-macarthurs-anti-social-justice-statement.html.

"Social Gospel." https://www.britannica.com/event/Social-Gospel.

Sowell, Thomas. *Black Rednecks and White Liberals*. New York: Encounter, 2005.

———. *Controversial Essays*. Stanford: Hoover Institution, 2002.

———. *Wealth, Poverty, and Politics*. New York: Basic, 2016.

"Stay Woke." https://www.merriam-webster.com/words-at-play/woke-meaning-origin.

Steele, Shelby. *White Guilt: How Blacks and Whites Together Destroyed the Promise of the Civil Rights Era*. New York: Harper Perennial, 2007.

Thatcher, Margaret. "Margaret Thatcher 1925–2013." https://www.oxfordreference.com/view/10.1093/acref/9780191843730.001.0001/q-oro-ed5-00010826.

Thenewcalvinist. "Stain of Mohler 3." *YouTube*, November 25, 2019. https://www.youtube.com/watch?v=MIlnLU-vt_g.

"What We Believe." https://web.archive.org/web/20200917194800/https://blacklivesmatter.com/what-we-believe/.

Williams, Jarvis J. "Biblical Steps Toward Removing the Stain." In *Removing the Stain of Racism from the Southern Baptist Convention*, edited by Jarvis J. Williams and Kevin M. Jones, 15–52. Nashville: B&H Academic, 2017.

Williams, Jarvis J., and Kevin M. Jones, eds. *Removing the Stain of Racism from the Southern Baptist Convention*. Nashville: B&H Academic, 2017.

Williams, Walter E. *Liberty Versus the Tyranny of Socialism: Controversial Essays*. Stanford: Hoover Institution Press, 2008.

———. *Race & Economics: How Much Can Be Blamed on Discrimination?* Stanford: Hoover Institution Press, 2011.

Witmer, John A. "Romans." In *The Bible Knowledge Commentary: An Exposition of the Scriptures*, edited by J. F. Walvoord and R. B. Zuck, 2:435–503. Wheaton, IL: Victor Books, 1985. Logos electronic edition.

Woods, Curtis A. "Are We There Yet? Concluding Thoughts About Removing the Stain of Racism from the Southern Baptist Convention." In *Removing the Stain of Racism from the Southern Baptist Convention*, edited by Jarvis J. Williams and Kevin M. Jones, 113–30. Nashville: B&H Academic, 2017.

Subject Index

Name Index

Scripture Index

Scripture Index

Joel

2:18—3:2	105

Amos

5:24	90

Micah

6:8	102, 145

Nahum

1:8–14; 2:1—3:19	105

Matthew

3:12	121
5:10–12, 44	102
5:27–28	102
5:27–28; 15:19	91
5:27–32	6, 31
5:43–44; 22:39	28
5:45	26
7:12	26
10:28	121
11:28–30	102
12:30–32	33
12:34; 15:38	31
12:41	70
15:18–19	83
15:18–20	6
15:21–28	110
16:18	98
18:11	77, 90, 122
19:19	102
22:37–39	114
22:39	102, 104
25:14–30	6, 26
28:18–20	102, 118

Mark

7:21	6, 31

Luke

5:32; 13:3	7
6:35	26
8:12	110
9:56	77, 122
12:16–22	25
13:3	102, 122
15:7; 17:3	70, 72
17:4; 24:47	71
17:11–17	26
23:34	77
23:43	77
24:47	77, 123

John

1:12	123
1:29	86, 104, 108, 113, 116, 122
1:29, 3:16	83
1:29; 3:16; 20:30–31	102, 145
3:1–4	6
3:1–4, 16	19, 31
3:1–7	90
3:1–14	116
3:3	70, 72, 85
3:3–8	103
3:16	17, 19, 26, 33, 72, 76, 86, 90, 93, 102, 104, 111, 123
3:16–18	108
3:17	102
3:18	92, 110, 118, 123
3:36; 6:40; 11:25–26	102
4:8	101
4:22	6, 117
8:32; 19:35; 20:30–31	22
12:35–36	7
14:6	22
17:17	22, 57, 101
20:31	123

Acts

2:21	110
2:38	77
2:38; 3:13; 10:43	71
10:10–16	120
10:34	101, 145
10:43	77, 123
11:18	120

Scripture Index